By the Few
for the Few

By the Few
for the Few

The Reagan Welfare Legacy

Tom Joe
The Center for the Study
of Social Policy

Cheryl Rogers
The Center for the Study
of Social Policy

Lexington Books
D.C. Heath and Company/Lexington, Massachusetts/Toronto

Library of Congress Cataloging in Publication Data
Joe, Tom.
  By the few for the few.

  Includes index.
    1. United States—Social policy—1980–
  2. Income maintenance programs—United States.   3. Public welfare
  —Georgia—Case studies.   4. United States—Politics
  and government—1981–   . I. Rogers, Cheryl.
  II. Title.
  HV95.J64   1985   361.6'1'0973   84–40827
  ISBN 0–669–10125–7 (alk. paper)
  ISBN 0–669–10167–2 (pbk. : alk. paper)

Published simultaneously in Canada
Printed in the United States of America on acid-free paper
Casebound International Standard Book Number: 0–669–10125–7
Paperbound International Standard Book Number: 0–669–10167–2
Library of Congress Catalog Card Number: 84–40827

Contents

Tables

Figures

Foreword

J
oseph Califano, former secretary of the Department of Health, Education, and Welfare, once called welfare the Middle East of domestic politics. It is at least as complicated, and almost as emotional. One of the coauthors of this very valuable book, Tom Joe, has been both in the trenches and the war rooms of the major front in the war on poverty for about 25 years. Yet this book is a new kind of venture for him, his coauthor, Cheryl Rogers, and their associates at the Center for the Study of Social Policy. Until now they have concentrated on being at the right place at the right time with fresh and relevant analyses of public policy issues. They have considered such issues in larger contexts—whether in the process of lawmaking or regulation-writing, or in getting the work done.

Here, however, Joe and Rogers have taken a step back, to reflect on where the Reagan revolution has moved both the theory and practice of helping the poor and disadvantaged in this country, and to speculate on the broad outlines of a counterrevolution. To sketch the book's conclusions and recommendations here would be a disservice to the cumulative power of a lot of gritty, disturbing facts and careful mounting of evidence. The authors suggest that the anecdotes upon which some of our present policies seem to be based and sold are more fraudulent than the fraud they were used to portray. Tom Joe knows intimately the long, winding trail of shifting federal policy intentions through statehouses, courthouses, and city halls to the actual delivery of checks and services. Hence, the book is able to show us the differences between stated intent and real outcomes in individual cases and families, as well as collectively. Here, if you will, are the real stories rather than anecdotal myths, the truth of discrete, disaggregated apples and oranges as against the simplistic and deceptive aggregations of lemons and passion fruit sometimes offered by the current administration.

None of us who knows the realities of the welfare past wants to go back to the way it was. There indeed was much that was wrong or counterproductive before Reagan, and the book's authors, working with previous administrations of both parties, participated in a series of welfare reform efforts. In fact, in looking at what has happened in the last four years, the book presents a case for what may be a central opportunity. The Reagan years have separated the problems of the nonworking poor and the working poor. The Joe–Rogers analysis argues that both have suffered, but only the working poor have been abandoned. All right, they contend, this means it is now possible to have a carefully articulated, new, and different program designed to help those working people who have been slipping under the poverty line in distressing and ever-increasing numbers. The patching and repositioning of the Reagan safety net for the nonworking poor needs attention, but it can be handled on a largely separate basis. The critical task, this book suggests, is addressing the often desperate problems of the working poor, problems of health, of hunger, and of incentives to keep on struggling upward out of poverty.

Most social policy insiders already know and respect Tom Joe. He isn't like anybody else, either in the variety and intensity of his experiences or in his special knowledge and competence. He is a unique resource, a policy analyst who has lived in the midst of the messy realities of the problem at state and local levels as well as in the White House, the Congress, and the once and perhaps future Department of Health, Education, and Welfare. Tom Joe has worked with and for Republicans and Democrats, executive- and legislative-branch staff and policymakers, local and nonprofit operators in the field, management, unions and professional associations, welfare rights advocates, and budget cutters. He has worked with one allegiance: to give the poor the greatest incentive and the best opportunity to escape both poverty and dependence, and to assure those who fall that their plight will not be ignored.

I hope this book extends the insiders' respect for Joe to a larger audience, and that this will permit him to make an even greater difference. And I further hope that aspiring policy analysts and program evaluators among this book's readers will emulate this model in the future. They will end up with dirtier fingernails and less elegant analyses, but they will make better contributions to the public weal.

Hale Champion
Executive Dean
John F. Kennedy School
of Government
Harvard University

Preface and Acknowledgments

In 1981, President Reagan proposed and the Congress enacted a set of sweeping policy changes and budget cuts in AFDC, the basic cash-assistance program for poor families. With the announcement of the proposed cuts, the Center for the Study of Social Policy began a study that spanned four years and traced the new policies from their inception through their enactment and implementation. The center's study, funded by the Ford Foundation and the Field Foundation, contained several components which together provide an in-depth spotlight on the government policy process.

We began somewhat inquisitively in 1981—when the welfare policy changes were first announced—by calculating their effects on typical family incomes. We then followed the legislative process through which Congress enacted them. One year later, we visited welfare offices in ten states to find out how the new policies were implemented and what effect they had had on state caseloads and budgets. To assess local implementation, we visited twenty-three county welfare offices in Georgia, reviewing case records and talking to local caseworkers. Finally, we interviewed 207 working-poor families in Georgia who had had their welfare benefits terminated as a result of the federal policies.

In some ways, the 1981 policy changes are over and done with. Hundreds of thousands of lives have been affected, and what was once new is now the norm. Our purpose here is not simply to reiterate the events of this period, but to help develop a better understanding of how government policies are developed, enacted, and implemented, with an eye toward improving this process in the future.

Acknowledgments

This book actually had many authors and an even greater number of reviewers. Although we cannot list them all here, we do want to acknowledge two colleagues: Peter Yu, for adding color and a sense of balance; and Mary Banks, without whose help this book would not have come about.

Introduction

This is a book about government, its capacities and its shortcomings, its success and its failures. Together, the chapters depict the essence of government—the human decisions and choices made daily that directly affect millions of people. The words show that government is far more than an automated, mechanical, predetermined system; instead it is driven by human insight, foibles, and occasionally, genius.

When we think of government, we generally do not think of its human qualities; we think of its institutions, born from traditions, agencies, and programs. This book is about some of these institutions. It touches on the legislative budget process, the politics of the executive branch, the federal-state "partnership" of a grant-in-aid program, and the local pulse of service delivery.

But government and its institutions must have a subject, for they do not exist in and of themselves. The subject of this book, then, is poverty, or, more precisely, poor people. These families—their lives, aspirations, and frustrations—make up the heart of the book, its raison d'être. In short, we try to show how poor people are ultimately affected by government and its institutions.

The particular government program addressed in this book is Aid to Families with Dependent Children (AFDC), the nation's primary cash-assistance program for low-income families. In 1981, a set of policy changes was enacted that constituted a radical departure from past policy. These changes provide the vehicle for examining government policy-making and implementation.

Execution of the federal government's 1981 AFDC policy changes was a little like changing a tire on a moving automobile. Nothing slowed down for the occasion. Moreover, to press the analogy further, the federal government managed not only to change the tire on a moving car but also to change the car's direction. This book reflects an interest in both the tire-changing antics and the substantive shift in the direction of public policy toward the poor.

The specific subjects of the book are working-poor families headed by single women. These are families living on the edge, not as desperately poor as some with no income, but still in poverty, daily struggling with the stark realities of economic hardship. These are people trying to raise themselves out of poverty by working. How we treat them is a crucial matter of governance.

This book describes a vertical process of government with respect to the AFDC policy changes of 1981. It analyzes the system from the beginning of a policy to its end, from ideology to reality. It explores who makes decisions, how they are made, how decisions are put into practice, and what impact they have. The story begins within the confines of the White House and the Office of Management and Budget; it proceeds through the corridors of Congress, in Washington, D.C.; to fifty state agencies; through various layers of federal and district courts, to thousands of local welfare offices throughout the country; and, eventually, to the individual families who were the ultimate targets of the policies. This process is far from simple or direct; it takes place within a tangle of government institutions and human dilemmas.

In tracing the flow of a particular set of public policies, this book provides a glimpse into the policy-making process from several vantage points. We try to get behind the AFDC changes to view them from the perspectives of several groups. We explore the administration's philosophy behind the changes, the reaction from interest and research organizations, congressional responses, the problems that state and local governments saw in trying to implement the new rules, and the caseworkers' and recipients' feelings about their effects. This perspective is important, as it conveys the tension and differences that are integral parts of the government policy process.

The book is divided into four parts. In part I, "The Context," we provide a framework for viewing the controversial AFDC policy changes. Chapter 1 briefly explores some of the dimensions of poverty—whom it affects, how it is measured, and what some of its causes are. Chapter 2 provides a brief history of government's responses to poverty and a more detailed overview of the structure of AFDC. In order to understand the importance of President Reagan's 1981 AFDC changes, both in theory and practice, it is necessary to understand the basic structure of the AFDC program. Without this understanding, the changes look like technical corrections of minor importance. This is a critical point because we often fail to understand a program's structural complexities and, as a result, we cannot gauge the impact of proposed "reforms."

Part II, "Policy Enactment and Implementation," takes an in-depth look at the 1981 AFDC amendments enacted as part of the Omnibus Budget Reconciliation Act (OBRA). Chapter 3 describes the administration's proposed AFDC changes and assesses public reaction to the plans. Chapter 4 analyzes the federal budget process and shows how the changes were enacted into law in 1981. Because a policy change merely begins with legislative enactment, chapters 5 and 6 take a closer look at the intergovernmental implementation process. Chapter 5 examines state actions both to implement and minimize the effects of the OBRA amendments. Chapter 6 investigates implementation of OBRA at the local level and uses a case study to illustrate the practical and human problems of translating federal law into practice.

The most neglected part of the policy process is a timely assessment of the effects of planned change. Unfortunately, we rarely learn from our mistakes because all too often we begin a new series of changes before knowing the results of past ones. Part III, "Effects," addresses this problem by presenting research evidence on the effects of the 1981 AFDC changes. The AFDC changes, in part because they produced so much controversy, were subject to much scrutiny. Chapter 7 summarizes the findings from several major studies on the impact of the new law. Chapter 8 offers an in-depth look at the effects of the changes on a sample of working women in Georgia who were terminated from AFDC because of OBRA. The Georgia study is significant because it goes beyond the statistics to the human impact on mothers and their children.

A detailed analysis of the 1981 AFDC changes is useful only to the extent that lessons are learned from the experience. Part IV, "Lessons for the Future," synthesizes the conclusions that emerged from the OBRA experience and suggests alternative paths for helping low-income families in the future. Chapter 9 summarizes the results of OBRA and outlines the major lessons of its implementation. Chapter 10 points out the need to move beyond budget cuts to more positive strategies to assist the working poor. Four short-term reforms are suggested. In chapter 11, a case is made for developing long-range strategies to prevent poverty as well as an agenda for more immediate policy reforms. This section is predicated on the belief that government, with all the expertise available to it, can and should do a better job of ameliorating and preventing poverty in the future than it has in the past.

Part I
The Context

1
The Problem of Poverty

The presence of poverty is not new and is not unique to the United States. There have been poor people as long as there has been property. But while the existence of poverty is old, the symptoms of poverty take on different forms in each society. The condition persists, but the faces, the reasons, the lives of poverty change. And although there are certain standard responses, each society deals with the problems of poverty differently.

In the United States, poverty has developed its own shape, changing over time. Today there are poor people in almost every community. There are also hard-core pockets of poverty among blacks and Hispanics in central cities, among white residents of Appalachia, among native Americans in communities in the Southwest, among farmers in the Midwest, and among a host of other families throughout the country. What binds these disparate families and individuals together is the lack of adequate income, the inability to secure basic necessities—food, clothing, and shelter—and the social and emotional isolation that such an economic condition conveys. Yet the very concept of poverty is elusive. Poverty eludes easy definition. Some see poverty as an absolute condition, associated with a medical or scientific standard—a tangible deficiency, such as malnutrition. Others see poverty as a relative condition, related to the distribution of wealth and resources in the society being considered. In this view, poverty is a severe inequity in the distribution of income and wealth. Those who favor an absolute definition might turn to an economic threshold tied to a medical or scientific standard. Those favoring a relative definition might establish a percentage of the average income as the poverty threshold—that is, everyone with income below, say, one-half the median income might be considered "poor."

There are advantages and disadvantages to each approach, and probably each is valid for different purposes. The official U.S. poverty standard is something of a hybrid of the two approaches. Developed in 1964 by the Social Security Administration as a means of counting poor persons, the standard is a partly absolute, partly relative estimate of the cost of a minimal standard of living. The absolute aspect consists of the Economy Food Plan—the cost of a "marketbasket" of food that constitutes a minimally nutritious diet. The relative aspect is the federal government's food expenditure survey of 1955, which found that American families spent about one-third of their income on food. (This is relative to other cultures and other periods of time, in which the percentage of income spent on food varies.) To derive the poverty threshold, the government then multiplied the cost of the food plan by three, reasoning that if a minimum diet costs X and food accounts for one-third of a family budget, then a minimum family budget is three times X.

Establishing a measure of poverty was not entirely scientific or precise; as a political act, it involved inevitable compromise, and as a pragmatic act, it was necessarily a very rough estimate based on a generalized set of circumstances. At the time the index was developed, there were at least two food plans from which to choose. Using the plan with the higher poverty threshold proved unacceptable because it would have meant that far too many people were poor. Government officials were worried they could not target aid on such a large number of poor. Instead, the government settled on the thrifty food plan which produced a more manageable number of poor people.[1] The official poverty threshold was thus established in 1965 and is still used today. The poverty standard was originally intended to be a rough measure by which to count the number of poor people in the nation. Its authors never anticipated that it would be used as a basis for programmatic and spending decisions. Yet the standard, which since 1965 has been adjusted annually to allow for price inflation, has been used to determine how much and what kind of help the government will provide for the poor. What started out as a method of counting the poor became an administrative tool for setting policy.

Despite its hybrid nature, the official definition of poverty tends to draw criticism from both sides. Some criticize the standard as too high, wishing it were more closely tied to the subsistence diet. Others argue the standard is too low, noting that while the standard is adjusted for inflation, it has not been adjusted for changes in consumption patterns.

Yet even if one accepts the federal government's definition of poverty, there still remains a question of how one defines income in determining how many people are poor. The official poverty measurements are based on cash income, that is, any family with a cash income below the poverty threshold is considered poor. Some low-income individuals and families, however, have access to free or reduced-cost services that are designed to improve the quality of their lives. The most significant among these are food stamps, Medicaid, and subsidized housing. Some argue that these "in-kind benefits" should be counted as income when measuring poverty, since they contribute to the resources of families. Measuring the cash value of these resources is, however, difficult. Over the years, there have been several attempts to place a dollar value on in-kind benefit programs and to alter the official U.S. definition of income.[2] This task is difficult when one tries to place a cash-dollar value on Medicaid, in particular, because the more one uses Medicaid, the more benefits one receives. Thus the sicker one is, the richer one would be classified. This is, of course, absurd. Recently, the Census Bureau published nine alternative measurements of poverty using various definitions of income.[3] If the current definition of cash income-only stands, it will not be because it is perfect, but because of the difficulties in reaching consensus on any alternative.

The statistics of poverty, while extremely limited and sometimes distracting from the real problems of poverty, do offer an initial picture of who is poor. But quantifying the problem as we do in the following pages is only a beginning; we must then go beyond the numbers and try to understand the nature of poverty, its human faces, and its roots.

A Statistical Portrait of Poverty

Using the official poverty standard, 35.2 million Americans, or 15.2 percent of the noninstitutional population, lived in poverty in 1983.[4] The poverty threshold for a family of four in that same year was $10,178. Table 1–1 shows the poverty rate using the various income definitions discussed previously. Depending on which definition is used, the incidence of poverty can be as low as 10 percent of the population, when

Table 1–1
Poverty Rates under Various Income Definitions, 1983

Income Definition	Poverty Rate
Official definition (cash income only)	15.2%
Cash, food, and housing:	
"Market value approach"	13.8
"Recipient value approach"	14.0
"Poverty budget share value approach"	13.9
Cash, food, housing, and medical care[a]	
"Market value approach"	10.5
"Recipient value approach"	13.2
"Poverty budget share value approach"	12.9
Cash income less taxes[b]	16.4

Source: "Estimates of Poverty Including the Value of Non-Cash Benefits: 1983," Bureau of the Census, U.S. Department of Commerce, Technical Paper 52, August 1984.
[a]Care for noninstitutionalized persons only.
[b]For 1982 from unpublished CPS data, Bureau of the Census.

Medicaid spending is counted, or as high as 16.4 percent, when only net cash income is counted.

Since 1960 (the first year for which statistics are available), the poverty rate has followed something of a roller-coaster path. As figure 1–1 shows, the rate has dropped fairly steadily from 1960 (22.2 percent) to 1973 (11.1 percent), its lowest level in American history. During the mid-1970s, the poverty rate remained at a fairly constant level. Since 1978, however, it has increased to 15.2 percent of the population. In other words, there was a 30 percent increase in the poverty rate between 1978 and 1983.

The actual number of people defined as poor has followed a similar path. Table 1–2 shows a steady and major decline in the number of poor people from 1960, when nearly 40 million people were "officially" poor, until 1978, when the number of people in poverty hit a low of 24.5 million. Since 1978, the number of people in poverty has grown to 35.2 million.

The poverty standard, while a useful tool, is ultimately somewhat arbitrary. The concept limits the difference between being poor and not being poor to only one dollar in income. Thus, a family of four whose 1983 income was $10,177 would be considered poor, while a similar family whose income was $10,179 would not officially be considered poor. There are a large number of "near-poor" Americans—that is, per-

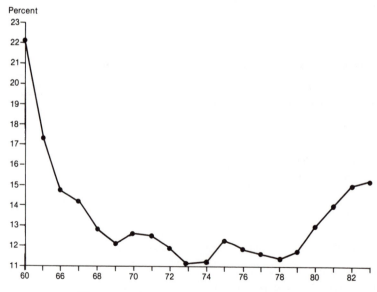

Figure 1–1. Poverty Rates, 1960–83

Table 1–2
The Population below the Poverty Line, 1960–83
(in millions)

Year	Number of Persons below Poverty Line
1960	39.9
1965	33.2
1970	25.4
1975	25.9
1976	25.0
1977	24.7
1978	24.5
1979	26.1
1980	29.3
1981	31.9
1982	34.4
1983	35.2

Source: *Money Income and Poverty Status of Families and Persons in the U.S.;* Current Population Reports, Consumer Income Series P-60, No. 145, Bureau of the Census, U.S. Department of Commerce, August 1984.

Note: This table measures only cash income in counting the number of people in poverty.

sons with incomes between 100 and 125 percent of the poverty threshold. If we increase the threshold by this 25 percent figure, the number of the poor increases by 35 percent.[5] Thus, although many have a tendency to speak of poverty as an all-or-nothing condition, there are, in fact, millions of people not considered poor whose standard of living is indistinguishable from the "official" poor.

Even when one's income falls below the poverty threshold, it can vary from as little as zero to as much as the $10,177 for a family of four. Thirty-seven percent of the poor have incomes that are less than 50 percent of the poverty threshold.[6] In 1983, this cutoff was $4,000 for a family of three, $5,090 for a family of four. Some of the poor are living with shockingly little money. It is difficult even to imagine how a family of three could live on $4,000 per year, or only $333 per month, in 1983. Clearly, there are large income differences even among those officially designated as poor.

Not only is poverty a broader phenomenon than most people believe, but there is substantial evidence that the gap between the rich and the poor is widening. A quiet economic polarization of American society has recently begun: over the past dozen years the number of rich *and* the number of poor Americans have increased while the number of middle-income households is diminishing. In 1970, 53 percent of all families had incomes between $15,000 and $35,000; in 1983, that figure had dropped

to 43 percent (in constant 1983 dollars). Of those families whose incomes were no longer in the median range, half entered the low income
bracket, with incomes of less than $15,000, and half went to the $35,000-
plus bracket.[7]

Most poverty data, as reported above, are based on single-year statistics. But a single year's data do not depict the fact that poverty is
dynamic and often temporary. People move in and out of poverty on a
frequent basis. While 35 million people may be poor each year, they are
seldom the same 35 million people from one year to the next. The Panel
Study of Income Dynamics (PSID) undertaken at the University of Michigan found that one-third to one-half of those who are poor in one year
are not poor in the next.[8] In fact, the study estimates that at least one-
quarter of the American population will live in poverty for at least one
year out of the next ten. Yet the PSID findings were based on data from
1967 to 1976—a relatively prosperous economic period. Given the more
recent tumultuous activity of the economy, the turnover in poverty today
is likely to be even higher than the PSID estimate.

In some ways, this is not surprising. Each of us is financially vulnerable, whether through job layoff, serious illness, divorce, or other events.
Over the course of time, poverty has many faces and the face of poverty
may, once in a while, be our own.

This is not to suggest that all poor people are poor for only a short
period of time. There is also a group of people who, although fewer in
number, are poor for long periods. For these families, poverty has become its own trap and they have no way to escape. Some of these families
remain poor all their lives.

The Faces of Poverty

In some ways, referring to the low-income population as "the poor" is
an unfortunate shorthand. It confers a single, often negative identity to
individuals who may have very little else in common:

> The faces of poverty are many and varied. At the most essential level
> we are talking about people: Weary young faces, and buoyant old ones.
> Children in patched, spotless dresses, and children covered with grime.
> Blacks, whites, native Americans. Speakers of "spanglish," Black En-
> glish, broken English, and the King's English. All of these people are in
> the gallery of poverty's faces.[9]

If all persons were photographed with a wide-angle lens, the viewer
would probably be surprised by the striking differences in the faces.

About one in ten of all the poor in the photograph would be elderly—65 years or older; about one in eight (13 percent) would be a nonelderly unrelated individual, that is, not living with other family members; one in three (33 percent) would be living in a family headed by a nonelderly single woman; and the remainder (43 percent) would be children and adults living in nonelderly married-couple families.[10]

If we look more closely at each of the subgroups, the picture is even more revealing. As table 1–3 shows, the poverty rate varies greatly from group to group. The highest rate is for families headed by single black women (53.8 percent); the lowest rate is for white married-couple families (8.1 percent).

The question of who is poor is inextricably linked to the question of why some people are poor. These questions are especially difficult to answer because there may be almost as many reasons for poverty as there are poor people.

> Some are poor because nature betrayed them at birth; others because a textile plant moved to Taiwan. Some are poor because they were not taught, others because they did not study. Still others . . . because men have oppressed women . . . whites have enslaved nonwhites . . . Some are poor despite unending virtue, work and toil; a few because they revel in sloth, cunning and artifice.[11]

Most people recognize that unwise individual choices, as well as social and economic factors beyond an individual's control, play roles in causing poverty. There is no easy way to confer blame for an individual's

Table 1–3
Poverty Rates for Selected Groups, 1983

Group	All Races	Black	White
All persons	15.2%	35.7%	12.1%
65+	14.1	35.7	12.0
<18	21.7	46.3	16.9
Families	12.3	32.4	9.7
Married-couple	7.6	16.2	8.1
Female-headed	36.0	53.8	28.3
Residence:			
Nonfarm	15.0	35.7	11.8
Farm	23.7	55.7	22.9
In central cities	19.8	37.0	14.1

Source: *Money Income and Poverty Status of Families and Persons in the U.S.;* Current Population Reports, Consumer Income Series P-60 no. 145, Bureau of the Census, U.S. Department of Commerce, August 1984.

poverty. While poverty is a personal economic condition, it is sometimes caused by macroeconomic conditions. There is a strong correlation between the poverty rate and the unemployment rate (see figure 1–2) and a strong, inverse correlation between the poverty rate and median family income nationwide (see figure 1–3). Recessionary periods in 1970, 1974–75, and 1980–82 can be seen in increased unemployment, reduced family income, and increased poverty. Thus, while we sometimes speak of poverty as a problem of the individual, of his or her personal deficiencies, at least part of the poverty problem is macroeconomic and beyond the individual's control.

For our purposes, the last quarter century can be divided roughly into two periods, 1960 to 1973 and 1973 to 1984. The first period was one of significant economic growth and expansion of social programs; there were no recessions during the 1960s. Unemployment fell to 4 percent in 1969 before increasing slightly during the 1970–71 recession. More important, family income grew in real terms. Over this period, poverty dropped from 22.2 percent in 1960 to 11.1 percent in 1973.

The second period—since 1973—has been dominated by two six-year cycles of inflation, recession, and recovery. The first cycle began with OPEC price increases in 1973; the second with similar increases in 1979. Both cycles clearly affected unemployment, family income, and

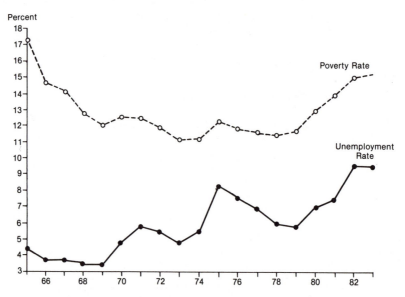

Figure 1–2. Poverty and Unemployment, 1965–83

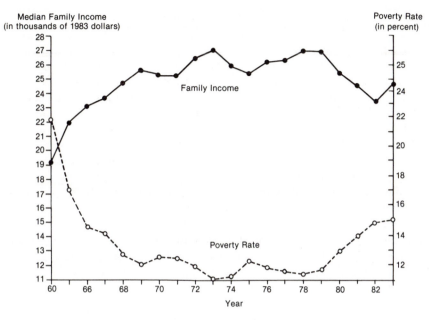

Figure 1–3. Family Income and Poverty, 1960–83

poverty. In 1983, just after the end of the 1980–82 recession, the poverty rate reached 15.2 percent—a nineteen-year high.

Different subgroups of the poor are affected by macroeconomic forces in different ways. For instance, poverty among married-couple families is very sensitive to changes in unemployment. During the 1980–82 recession, more than one million of these families lost their jobs and fell into poverty; these families are the often-cited "new poor." Even more than for other families, the poverty rate for married-couple families closely mirrors the unemployment rate. Poverty among the elderly is less sensitive to unemployment, since few of the elderly are employed. When the overall poverty rate rose in 1970 and 1981–82 because of increased unemployment, the elderly poverty rate either declined or remained steady, owing in large measure to Social Security.

Families headed by single women are doubly vulnerable to macroeconomic forces. The poverty rate for these families is sensitive to unemployment. Moreover, millions of these families also receive public assistance, and rapid inflation devalues their fixed incomes. Between 1978 and 1982, poverty among female-headed families increased by 30 percent.

Yet even in prosperous economic periods, there are poor people.

Many people are poor because of their weak attachment to the labor force. In 1983, nearly 50 percent of all poor people worked for at least some part of the year. These people work but cannot raise themselves or their families above poverty. Often they can find only part-time jobs; or, if they are single parents, they can afford only part-time jobs while their children are in school; or they work for only part of the year and are unable to find another job after being laid off. Even those who work full-time cannot always command a salary sufficient to raise them out of poverty. The unspoken secret about the American dream is that one can work hard and still be poor. The poverty threshold for a family of three is $8,460, but if one worked all year long at a minimum-wage job, as many do, one would earn $6,968 in *gross* wages, only 82 percent of the poverty threshold for a family of three.

Macroeconomic forces are not always the cause of poverty; other less tangible roots are also at play. Individuals and families may be poor because of a lack of marketable skills, a lack of motivation, a recent divorce or separation, retirement, old age, or an illness. Many of these causes are not assessed in the surveys that measure poverty.

A Special Problem: Female-Headed Families

Female-headed families are of particular concern. The incidence of poverty among them is extremely high—about six times the rate for married-couple families. Moreover, poverty among these families is directly tied to family structure and is particularly intractable. Single mothers do not have the luxury of staying home with their children while a spouse earns money. If they work, they must pay for day care for their young children; if they do not work, they will remain poor. It is not surprising that poverty is so widespread among female-headed families.

Even in an economic peak period such as 1978, 31.5 percent of all female-headed families lived in poverty (see figure 1–4). The contrasting poverty rate for married-couple families in 1978 was 5.3 percent. As with other groups, employment status is the prime determinant of poverty among female-headed families. The poverty rate for families headed by women who held full-time, year-round jobs was 6 percent; for families headed by women who did not work at all, it was 57 percent.[12]

These numbers should not be misconstrued to mean that women who head families are less willing to work than women who do not. In fact, women who head families are more likely to work than either women in married-couple families or women without children. More than 59

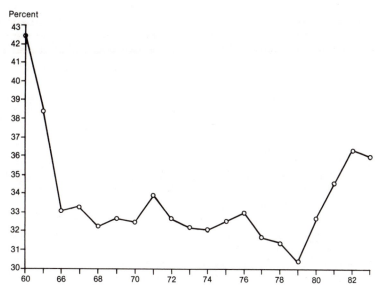

Figure 1–4. Poverty Rate among Female-Headed Families

percent of these single mothers work, compared to 47 percent of all married mothers.[13] The difference is that for single mothers not working means economic hardship.

This intractability is more troubling given the dramatic increase in female-headed families. Since 1960, the number of female-headed families has doubled, whereas the number of married-couple families has increased by only 20 percent. Thus, while the poverty rate for married-couple families has stayed roughly constant, the number of poor female-headed families has increased. Although persons in these families make up only 13 percent of the population, they constitute 34 percent of the poverty population.

What does it mean, then, to be poor? Sometimes it seems that impoverishment has taken on an abstract statistical meaning, that destitution has been reduced to a set of moving numbers, alternately producing headlines such as "Poverty on the Rise" or "Poverty Dips." Yet forcibly fitting a human dilemma like poverty into bar graphs and pie charts falls short of what is needed for a complete understanding of the issue.

Poverty is a complex social and economic condition that has as its roots a host of both macroeconomic and personal forces. Its faces and causes are as varied as any cross section of Americans, spanning all ages, races, and religions and cropping up in almost every locale in the country. It is much more than a statistical phenomenon; it is a human condition that has been with us since our country was founded and that continues to define too large a portion of our national citizenry.

Notes

1. Leonard Beeghley, *Living Poorly in America* (New York: Praeger Publishers, 1983), 18–19.
2. See, for example, Timothy Smeeding, *Alternative Methods for Valuing Selected In-kind Transfer Benefits and Measuring Their Effect on Poverty,* Washington, D.C.: U.S. Bureau of the Census, 1982.
3. *Estimates of Poverty Including the Value of Non-Cash Benefits: 1983,* Washington, D.C.: U.S. Bureau of the Census, U.S. Department of Commerce, Technical Paper 52, August 1984.
4. *Money Income and Poverty Status of Families and Persons in the United States: 1983,* Current Population Reports, Consumer Income Series P-60 no. 145, Bureau of the Census, U.S. Department of Commerce, August 1984.
5. Unpublished data from the 1984 Current Population Survey, Bureau of the Census.
6. Ibid.
7. Ibid.
8. Greg J. Duncan, *Years of Poverty, Years of Plenty* (Ann Arbor: The Institute for Social Research, University of Michigan, 1984).
9. Manuel Carballo and Mary Jo Bane, *The State and the Poor in the 1980's* (Boston: Auburn House Publishing Co., 1984), xviii.
10. Bureau of the Census, *Money Income and Poverty Status.*
11. Carballo and Bane, *State and the Poor,* xviii.
12. Bureau of the Census, *Money Income and Poverty Status.*
13. *Perspectives on Working Women: A Databook,* Bureau of Labor Statistics, U.S. Department of Labor, Bulletin 2080, October 1980, derived from tables 68 and 81.

2
Government's Response to Poverty

S ociety's response to poverty has a long and rich history. Several texts describe this history in detail, a task which is beyond the scope of this book. However, it is useful to note some of the major historical antipoverty interventions in this country and the premises about poverty upon which they were based. This chapter briefly explores the major responses to poverty in the United States, with particular focus on the evolution of AFDC and an overview of its current structure. This material provides a context for viewing the AFDC policy changes of 1981 as described in chapter 3.

American treatment of the poor has its foundations in the Elizabethan Poor Laws of sixteenth-century England. These laws gave local jurisdications the power to raise taxes in order to build almshouses, which were little more than shacks for the poor; to supply sustenance to the aged, handicapped, and other helpless groups in their own homes; and to purchase materials with which to put "vagrants" and other able-bodied unemployed persons to work. Occasionally, poor persons were indentured to respectable citizens for a period of one year, during which they worked for the host in return for room and board. During the settlement of the thirteen colonies that were to become the United States, these laws prevailed.

During the eighteenth and nineteenth centuries, poor persons, called "paupers," were believed to be individually guilty for their poverty. Poverty was viewed as a disgrace and the poor person as lazy and incompetent. It was assumed that the poor could get work if they wanted it, so relief must be made as disagreeable as possible in order to discourage dependence.

Local government "aid," repressive as it was, continued as the sole response to poverty until the mid to late 1800s, when a parallel private charity movement was created. During this time, groups of citizens began to react against local government relief to the poor. Citizens distrusted and even feared the harsh and punitive methods used in administering local aid. Corruption was rife. Out of this dissatisfaction grew a social welfare movement in the private sector that was based on the desire to rehabilitate individuals. It became common to view the impoverished person as someone who needed care and attention in order to become motivated and capable of being self-sufficient. Poverty was seen as the result of individual malfunctioning. Social workers attempted to provide moral encouragement and serve as models to the poor rather than give material assistance. While trying to rehabilitate the poor through "magnanimity and concern and personal touch of the friendly visitor," they demonstrated their moralistic attitude by denying the poor more tangible aid.[1] Social workers would tell clients what they should eat and wear, how and where they should live, and how they should arrange their relationships with others. In short, it was the social worker's duty not to loan money or buy a poor person a new pair of shoes, but to impart morality.

By the early 1900s, one group considered particularly "deserving"— widowed mothers—was singled out by states and localities for special aid. It was not fair, so reformers claimed, that such needy persons be blamed for their poverty, labeled paupers, and placed in almshouses. Instead, it was argued, these persons should be provided "pensions" without humiliating investigation and stigma. Between 1910 and 1926, all but six states enacted Mothers' Pension programs. At first, only widows with children were eligible, but by 1926, eligibility was generally expanded to include mothers who were divorced or whose husbands were dead, had deserted them, become totally incapacitated, or gone to prison.

There were several limitations, however, to the Mothers' Pension programs. For one, the assistance payments were so low—generally $20 to $50 per month—that most recipients worked as housekeepers or took in laundry to supplement the public assistance. Second, the programs were optional to cities and counties within the state. As a result, many localities, especially small towns, did not provide aid to widowed mothers. But Mothers' Pensions (as well as pensions for the aged poor, which were also developed during this period) were clear attempts to help the deserving poor through cash assistance.

This system of local public and private aid prevailed until the depression of 1929–33 when, suddenly, the ranks of the unemployed swelled. By 1933, some 15 million people, or 12 percent of the total population, had lost their jobs.[2] The problems of unemployment and poverty were for the first time seen as national in scope and therefore as a legitimate concern of the federal government. State and local governments could no longer afford to support all those in need within their jurisdictions. The federal government's initial response was to offer temporary emergency relief and to create massive jobs programs. Congress enacted the Federal Emergency Relief Act (FERA) in 1933 to provide cash to the poorest families, and appropriated $500 million to the states to help "relieve the hardship and suffering caused by unemployment."[3] Thus the federal government had become a financier; states and localities decided who was to get how much money, surplus commodities, and medical care.

Two years later, President Roosevelt presented plans for a jobs program designed to replace the relief provided through FERA. It was generally agreed that continued dependence on relief was destructive to the human spirit and that jobs for the able-bodied must be provided. The Works Progress Administration (WPA) was created to finance "small useful projects" for the needy unemployed who were on relief.

Yet officials dissatisfied with the concept of temporary relief as embodied in FERA wanted to devise a more permanent solution to the problems associated with poverty. The Social Security Act of 1935, the centerpiece of President Roosevelt's New Deal, grew out of this desire to protect people from unemployment, poverty, and income loss on a long-term basis as well as in the short run following the depression. At the time, only about 15 percent of all employed people held jobs covered by any sort of retirement system, and only a tiny handful—fewer than 1 percent—were actually receiving a pension. It was almost inevitable that one would reach the poorhouse toward the end of one's life.

The Social Security Act provided protection from loss of income due to retirement through the Federal System of Old Age Insurance benefits, financed by employers and employees. It also provided for unemployment compensation through insurance funds set aside by employers. In both programs, benefits are paid to legally entitled contributors who have worked and earned their right to receive benefits when they become unemployed or retired. Over the years the Old Age Insurance system was expanded to include dependents and survivors of covered workers, the disabled, farmers, and government and nonprofit workers, as well as to provide medical care for older people and disabled persons.

But the designers of the Social Security Act recognized that insurance benefits earned through prior work could not meet all economic and social needs. They could protect against poverty due to temporary, involuntary unemployment or old age, but they did nothing for poverty resulting from other forces. Consequently, three special programs were created: Aid to Dependent Children (ADC), which provided federal funds for cash payments to children based on the state Mothers' Pension programs; Aid to the Blind; and Old Age Assistance for those who were either ineligible for Old Age Insurance or who were inadequately provided for by that program. These were "needs-tested" programs to assist specified groups; that is, to receive assistance, the applicant had to have income and assets below a specified level. This is in contrast to the social insurance programs, which paid benefits to all contributors regardless of their income. The needs-tested programs were initially intended to be temporary stopgaps that would wither away as a vigorous economy and a fully developed social insurance system made them unnecessary.

These latter programs were also designed as "entitlement" programs. This means that anyone who is eligible for benefits has a legal right to receive such benefits. The government cannot award benefits to some and deny benefits to others who have the same characteristics. All needy children as well as blind and elderly persons who met the eligibility requirements were "entitled" to receive benefits. States are required to provide all persons who wish to make application for aid with an opportunity to do so, to furnish aid promptly, and to provide for a hearing for those denied aid. This is in contrast to a program in which only certain applicants are allowed to participate and for which government can control the number of participants and set a fixed dollar ceiling on costs.

Aid to Dependent Children

At the time, little attention was paid to ADC, which was thought of as a relatively minor part of the Social Security Act compared to the social insurance programs. Under ADC, Title IV of the Social Security Act, Congress authorized funds "for the purpose of enabling each state to furnish financial assistance . . . to needy dependent children." The federal government paid one-third of the state benefit costs up to $6 for the first child and $4 for each additional child. The federal government left it up to the states to determine the definition of *need* but specified that children must be under age sixteen and must be deprived of parental support "by reason of death, continued absence from the house, or physical or mental incapacity of a parent."[4] For the first few years, ADC remained a small program. In 1938, there were only 935,000 children receiving benefits, and total program costs amounted to about $100 million.[5] As late as 1949, President Truman's Social Security administrator voiced the administration's view that ". . . this public assistance is a residual program to help needy persons who are not adequately protected by the various forms of contributory social insurance. . . . If we have a comprehensive contributory social insurance system . . . in time the residual load of public assistance would become so small in this country that the States and the localities could reasonably be expected to assume that load without federal financial participation."[6]

Yet over the next decade, several expansions in ADC and Social Security were made, and several new needs-tested programs were created. In ADC, the federal matching rate was increased several times. By

1948, the federal government paid $16.50 per month for the first child, and there were 1.4 million children receiving aid.[7]

In 1950, the program was broadened to permit the mother or other caretaker relative (such as an aunt or grandmother) living with the needy child to receive aid as well. The caseload jumped to over 2 million people.[8]

Also in 1950, Congress created a program to add disabled persons to Social Security's insurance plan. One year later it created a needs-tested program called Aid to the Permanently and Totally Disabled (APTD) for those not covered by the social insurance program for the disabled.

During the 1950s, a significant shift occurred in the composition of the public assistance caseload. As the number of aged persons declined, the number of single-parent families climbed. Moreover, the composition of the ADC caseload itself was changing. In 1936, the death of a parent was the single largest reason for receiving ADC. By 1960, 67 percent of those receiving ADC were dependent because the father was absent from the home on account of divorce, separation, imprisonment, or illegitimacy. Only 8 percent of the fathers were dead.

By 1960, the worthiness of the clients on public assistance was beginning to be called into question; 40 percent of all ADC clients were black, and families were staying on for longer periods of time. Racial tensions flared, the public became concerned about family breakdown, and ADC was blamed for encouraging immorality among the poor. Public outrage began to mount.

ADC was by no means withering away. On the contrary, caseloads were growing and costs were rising rapidly. When President Kennedy took office in 1961, ADC was becoming a major political liability. In 1961, President Kennedy developed a new federal law that allowed states to extend ADC benefits to two-parent families in which the father was unemployed. However, states were forbidden to aid the family if the unemployed parent refused to accept work without good cause. Few states implemented the new program at first. (By 1984, half of the states chose to exercise this option, yet the total number of two-parent families receiving benefits remains relatively small at less than 10 percent of all AFDC families nationwide.)

But the real change came in President Kennedy's special message to Congress on February 1, 1962. He stated that cash assistance was an insufficient solution to a set of complicated social and personal problems. Equally important, he claimed, was the need for services directed toward prevention and rehabilitation. Thus, the answer to the welfare problem in 1962 was services, which President Kennedy and others claimed would save money and rescue wasted lives.

On the same day that Kennedy made his speech, Wilbur Mills, chairman of the House Ways and Means Committee, introduced the Public Welfare Amendments of 1962. This legislation increased federal financial participation in the cost of services from 50 to 75 percent. Thus, for every dollar the state spent on services to ADC recipients, the federal government now paid 75 cents. Although "services" were never precisely defined, they were referred to as those designed to help recipients retain capability for self-care or to prevent or reduce dependency. The law also made a number of other changes, but they were minor in comparison to the new service thrust. The one other noteworthy change was that the name was altered to Aid to Families with Dependent Children (AFDC) to reflect the enlarged focus of the program.

In hindsight, it is easy to see that the 1962 amendments created unrealistic expectations. No one knew exactly what services to deliver, and the promise that rehabilitation would reduce the welfare rolls and their costs was not based on any evidence. However, at the time, there was great hope for the new strategy.

The 1962 AFDC amendments confirmed a growing tendency to try to root out and deal with the causes of poverty instead of merely granting financial assistance. During the next few years under President Lyndon Johnson, a counterstrategy was developed to combat poverty outside the established welfare system. During this time, public attention was drawn to the problem of poverty with Michael Harrington's now famous book *The Other America*. On March 16, 1964, President Johnson submitted legislation to Congress known as the Economic Opportunity Act (EOA). It became law that August and commenced the much-heralded War on Poverty.

The Economic Opportunity Act revolved around community action. Local councils made up of government officials, voluntary agency representatives, and poor persons themselves would develop an antipoverty plan specific to their locality, and the federal government would help finance it. It was that part of the act which provided for community action that made the legislation new and different from past efforts. The federal Office of Economic Opportunity (OEO) was created, and it funded Head Start, Upward Bound, day-care centers, health centers, and neighborhood legal centers, according to local requests.

Other titles of the act provided for education, training, and job opportunities for youth through the Job Corps and other programs; aid to rural and depressed areas through loans and tax credits; and a domestic counterpart to the Peace Corps: Volunteers in Service to America (VISTA). One billion dollars was spent in the first year, although half of that money was derived from already existing programs.

In addition to these efforts, bold new programs to provide goods and services to the poor were also established. Medicare, which pays for health care for the elderly and disabled, and Medicaid, which pays for health care for AFDC and other public-assistance recipients, were both born in 1965. The food stamp program, which sold reduced-price food coupons to low-income families, was created in 1968.

In some ways, these programs were an indictment of the public welfare system of the early 1960s. Officials were expressing their frustration that previous policies had not reduced poverty. New strategies were seen as necessary to combat the alarming growth in poverty.

In fact, the next legislative thrust involving AFDC was designed to get people off the welfare rolls by making them self-sufficient in the labor market. The 1967 Welfare Amendments, pushed by Wilbur Mills, largely restricted AFDC benefits and made mandatory a work-training program for all persons over sixteen years old receiving AFDC. To try to get people off the welfare rolls and into the job market, the 1967 amendments introduced a work incentive. Known technically as the "$30 plus one-third disregard," the provision allowed more working parents to remain eligible for partial AFDC grants. The theory was put forth that if government encouraged mothers to work by allowing them to keep a small AFDC payment, they would be more likely to work their way off the welfare rolls.

Only two years later, as welfare was continuing to become less and less popular, President Nixon submitted to Congress the Family Assistance Plan (FAP), which constituted the first national welfare reform debate. The proposal established a federal floor in AFDC, ensuring a minimum income for all eligible families. Although the plan did not pass both houses of Congress, it set the terms for the first national debate about how to target cash assistance to the poor. As part of the FAP debate, members of Congress learned about the nation's primary welfare program and participated in discussions about its principles and practices.

Congress did, however, pass one portion of FAP, creating the federally funded Supplemental Security Income (SSI) program. SSI replaced the Aid to the Blind, Old Age Assistance, and Aid to the Totally and Permanently Disabled programs, and provided a national minimum benefit for low-income elderly, blind, and disabled persons.

In 1973, Congress passed the Comprehensive Employment and Training Act (CETA). Through state and local agencies, CETA provided employment (mostly in the public sector) for disadvantaged persons. From the start, CETA had administrative difficulties. With the broad latitude given local administrators, there were complaints that CETA was inadequately targeted and that it often provided dead-end employment.

In 1975, Congress for the first time tried to address the problems of the working poor as opposed to those of the unemployed poor. Its vehicle was the tax system. By creating the Earned Income Tax Credit (EITC), Congress sought to assist low-wage workers. The EITC was designed to offset the payroll taxes that low-wage earners still had to pay even though they were poor. Under EITC in 1975, families who had children and who earned less than $8,000 per year were eligible to receive a tax credit of up to $400. The credit could be used to offset the family's tax liability or it could be paid to the family directly if there was no tax liability.

Despite all these efforts, poverty persisted. The last initiative on poverty reform before President Reagan took office in 1981 occurred in 1977, when the Carter administration revived the AFDC welfare-reform debate by introducing its Program for Better Jobs and Income (PBJI). PBJI combined a reform of the cash-assistance system with a major jobs-creation program, but it was defeated in Congress.

Meanwhile, the number of families receiving AFDC was continuing to grow. As figure 2–1 shows, the number of recipients grew at a steady but slow rate from 1935 to the late 1960s. The late sixties and early seventies saw a large increase in the AFDC caseload when benefits were expanded. In the six years between 1965 and 1971, the number of AFDC recipients doubled, reaching 9.7 million. This growth slowed and the

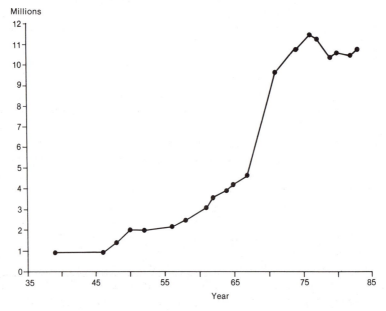

Figure 2–1. AFDC Recipients, 1939–83

AFDC caseload reached a peak of 11.5 million persons in 1976. Since that time, the caseload has leveled off near 10.5 million people. Since the mid-seventies AFDC benefit levels have been rapidly devalued by inflation; in real terms, the median state monthly AFDC benefit declined by 24 percent owing to inflation between 1975 and 1983.[9] AFDC is the only federal cash-assistance program that is not indexed to keep pace with inflation.

As can be seen, the sixties and seventies witnessed a surge in categorical antipoverty programs, each targeted to discrete needs and populations. Yet by 1980 there still remained many poor people who did not receive assistance, people who fell through some rather large cracks in the much touted "social safety net." Single individuals and childless couples did not qualify for AFDC, nor, in half the states, did married couples with children.

By 1980, it was safe to say that some of the antipoverty programs had worked—that is, had been successful in reducing poverty—while others had not. The most successful of all the programs was Social Security. Recognizing the problems of poverty among the retired and the disabled, Social Security was designed as a forward-looking program— one that anticipated income deficiencies and planned to avoid them. Without their Social Security benefits, it is estimated that over half of the elderly would have incomes below the official poverty standard instead of the less than 15 percent that lived below the poverty line in 1983. But poverty associated with retirement, death, or disability is easier to prevent than poverty associated with unemployment, undertraining, illegitimacy, or family breakup. Preventing the latter requires changing behavior or attitudes, or intervening extensively in the labor market— tasks which have proven extremely difficult for the federal government.

This brief history spanning two centuries shows that AFDC, the particular program examined in this book, is but one narrow band in the broad spectrum of antipoverty programs. Its shape evolved incrementally over the years as new directions were imposed on it. On the following pages we describe the structure of AFDC as it existed in 1980, after the failed welfare reform attempts led by Presidents Nixon and Carter and before President Reagan introduced his changes in 1981.

AFDC in 1980: An Overview

In 1980, 3.8 million families received AFDC at a cost to the federal and state governments of $12.8 billion. The following characteristics describe the families receiving aid:

The typical AFDC family consists of a mother and two children. In 1969, the average AFDC family size was four persons; today it is just under three persons.

More than 40 percent of the families are black; 52 percent are white.

Most AFDC families live in metropolitan areas. One in five AFDC families lives in Chicago, Detroit, Houston, Los Angeles, New York, or Philadelphia.

The average AFDC child is eight years old; 36 percent of AFDC children are under age six.

More than half of all AFDC mothers are under age 30; one-third are younger than 25.

These demographic characteristics provide an initial sense of the families receiving AFDC: they are young, disproportionately black mothers, with young children, usually living in a large city. Yet it is somewhat misleading to talk of the caseload as if it were static. Instead, many families move on and off the welfare rolls as employment and family situations change. One study found that over half of all AFDC families received assistance for less than one year. In addition, the study found that a smaller segment of the caseload stays on the rolls for an average of four to five years.[10] Thus, while the AFDC caseload may remain roughly constant from year to year, the people on AFDC in one year are not always the same as those who are on it the next year.

AFDC remains a joint federal-state program. The federal government sets broad eligibility guidelines and helps finance the program, and states are free to establish specific eligibility standards and benefit levels. The federal government pays at least 50 percent of each state's benefit payments and as much as 77 percent, depending on per-capita income in the state. For example, in states like New York, California, Connecticut, and Illinois, where per-capita income is high, the federal government pays 50 percent of all program costs. In states with low per-capita income, like South Carolina, Arkansas, and Mississippi, the federal government pays 70, 72 and 77 percent, respectively, of all benefits.

The federal-state partnership allows considerable discretion at the state level. As a result, eligibility and benefit levels vary greatly among states. The problem here is that benefits are far from adequate, and eligibility standards are very low in many states. Consider the following eligibility and benefit rules.

Determining whether a family qualifies for AFDC benefits is a four-step process. As figure 2–2 illustrates, a family must meet several requirements concerning family composition, assets, and income before benefits are awarded. Generally speaking, the applicant must be a single

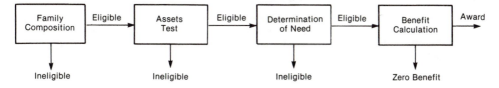

Figure 2–2. AFDC Eligibility

parent living with at least one child under age eighteen. (If the children are between the ages of eighteen and twenty-one, they must be full-time students.) In half the states, the applicant may be married, but the principal earner must be unemployed. In the other half, the applicant must be a single parent.

Each state also has its own assets test, with a federal limit of $2,000 in 1980. An applicant with assets (for instance, furniture, clothing, and savings, but excluding a house and one car) valued at more than $2,000 is ineligible. States, however, often impose stricter assets tests of their own. In Georgia, for example, a family is ineligible for AFDC if it has more than $800 in assets (excluding a house, furnishings, $1,000 face value of life insurance, and a car, if the car is at least four years old). If, for instance, the applicant has a savings account with more than $800 tucked away for her children's education, or a life insurance policy worth more than $1,000, or a relatively new car worth more than $800, her family is ineligible for aid.

If a family meets the composition and assets requirements, it then must be found to be in "need"—that is, with sufficiently low income to qualify for aid. There is no single, national "need standard" but rather fifty-one different AFDC need standards, or eligibility levels. In 1980, monthly need standards for a family of four ranged from $187, in Texas, to $753, in Vermont (see figure 2–3).

Need is determined by comparing family income to the state need standard. Each state establishes its own need standard, the amount deemed necessary by the state to meet minimal needs for food, clothing, and shelter. A family is ineligible if its income exceeds the need standard and is eligible if its income falls below the need standard. States also establish a payment standard (irrespective of the need standard) that determines the amount paid to an eligible family. Benefits are determined by comparing a family's income to a state payment standard. The difference between the two is the AFDC grant. Families with no income receive the full amount of the payment standard, and families with some income receive lesser grants. In about half the states, the need standard and the payment standard are the same; that is, the state pays the amount it

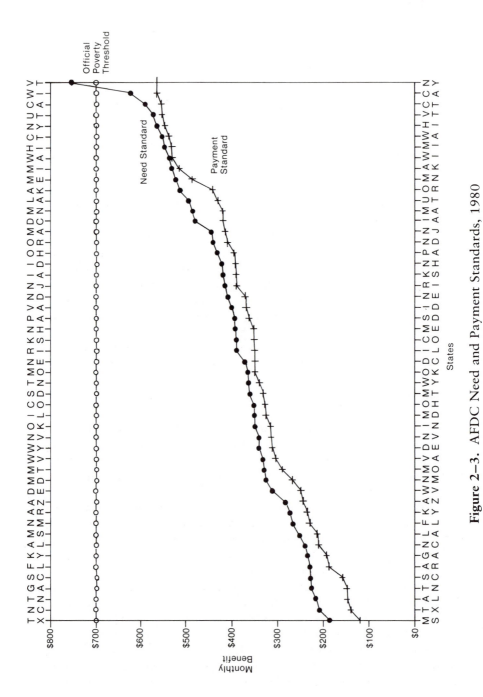

Figure 2–3. AFDC Need and Payment Standards, 1980

believes a family needs for subsistence. In the other half, however, the state pays only a portion of the need standard.

Before 1962, gross earnings were counted dollar for dollar against the state's eligibility and payment standard, so very few working families qualified for aid. In 1962, however, Congress required states to disregard reasonable work expenses, including taxes, uniforms, and transportation to and from work. Congress wanted to give working mothers an advantage on the premise that since work expenses were not available to the mothers as disposable income, such costs should not be counted as income for purposes of calculating AFDC eligibility and benefits. In other words, states could deduct only net earnings from the grant of a working family.

In a further step to provide a work incentive, Congress allowed a portion of the mother's net wages to be disregarded when calculating AFDC benefits. The first $30 of monthly earnings, plus one-third of the remainder, was made exempt. This lowered the amount of income attributed to a working family, thereby increasing its AFDC grant. This work incentive, enacted in 1967, was intended to make it more profitable for mothers on AFDC to work than not to work.

If a family passes all these eligibility tests, its AFDC benefits are calculated against the state payment standard. If the family's net income (minus disregards) is not below the payment standard, it does not receive a grant. If the net income *is* below the payment standard, the family receives a payment equal to the difference. Again, monthly benefit levels vary greatly from state to state. In 1980, maximum monthly benefits for a family of four ranged from $120 (or 14 percent of the poverty threshold) in Mississippi to $563 (or 80 percent of the poverty threshold) in California (see figure 2-3). In the median state, AFDC benefits amount to about half the poverty standard, and three-quarters of the states provide benefits at less than 65 percent of the poverty level. Even when AFDC benefits are combined with food stamps, as they often are, their combined value remains below the poverty level in all states except Alaska.

These data show that AFDC recipients must be poor before becoming eligible for AFDC, and that, once eligible, they still live well below the poverty standard. Moreover, the data show that AFDC is really a set of fifty-one different programs; eligibility and benefits are determined largely by where one happens to live. Thus there is no uniform national cash-assistance policy or minimum-benefit standard for nonelderly poor families, a fact that was almost changed by President Nixon's Family Assistance Plan but that has consistently evaded welfare reformers.

Once certified as eligible for AFDC, a family becomes automatically eligible for Medicaid and is thereby entitled to free medical care with any participating physician. Eligibility for Medicaid is tied directly to eligibility for cash assistance, which means that eligibility for Medicaid depends on state standards just as AFDC does. With some exceptions, to be eligible for Medicaid one must be eligible for AFDC or SSI. Conversely, losing AFDC eligibility means losing Medicaid coverage in twenty-one states. In the other twenty-nine states, plus the District of Columbia, a family must have large health bills in relation to its income to qualify for Medicaid.

In fiscal terms, however, Medicaid has far outgrown AFDC and SSI. In 1983, Medicaid expenditures totaled $32 billion more than AFDC ($13.4 billion) and SSI ($9.5 billion) combined. Only a small portion of Medicaid funds were spent on AFDC mothers and children; a large portion financed the long-term institutional care of elderly and disabled SSI recipients. Nevertheless, Medicaid is vitally important to the health of low-income families. Since many low-income working mothers neither receive health insurance for themselves and their children from their jobs nor earn enough money to pay for health insurance themselves, Medicaid is of vital concern to AFDC families. In fact, critics have often argued that the linkage between AFDC and Medicaid eligibility creates a work disincentive by discouraging mothers from working their way off AFDC because they fear losing essential health-care coverage for their families.

In addition to Medicaid, about three-quarters of all AFDC families also receive food stamps. The interaction between AFDC and food stamps is unique, because food stamp allotments are inversely related to family income, including AFDC. Thus, the higher a family's AFDC benefit, the lower its food stamp allotment, and vice versa.

Unlike AFDC and Medicaid, the food stamp program is funded and benefits are set by the federal government, which provides a uniform benefit throughout the country. The food stamp program is broader than AFDC: it does not limit eligibility to single parents, as AFDC does, and it has higher eligibility and benefit levels. In 1983, 22 million people— one out of ten Americans and twice as many as those on AFDC—received food stamps costing an average of $34 per person per month and a total of $12.7 billion.

Thus AFDC, Medicaid, and food stamps have evolved into an interlocking system that must be viewed in its entirety. All too often, each of them is dealt with separately since each has its own authorizing committee, executive agency, and line item in the federal budget. The linkage among the programs means that changes in one must account for effects on the others.

In summary, AFDC was created as a small adjunct to the Social Security program. It was intended to be a minor cash-assistance program for dependent children, never the major welfare program it has become. However, because there is no universal program for preventing poverty among families headed by women and other nonelderly families, AFDC has evolved into the main welfare program for the poor. It is within this context that President Reagan proposed a set of sweeping changes in the nation's needs-tested programs, and the most radical of these changes were in AFDC. A detailed examination of President Reagan's AFDC proposals, their legislative history, and multiple consequences is explored in the remainder of this book.

Notes

1. Harold Richman, *"Alms and Friends: the Relationship between Social Services and Financial Assistance in Public Welfare Policy,"* Ph.D. diss., University of Chicago, 1969.

2. Josephine C. Brown, *Public Relief 1929–1939* (New York: Henry Holt & Co., 1940)), 65.

3. Ibid., 146.

4. Title IV, Social Security Act of 1935.

5. Vee Burke, *Brief Legislative History of Title IV-A of the Social Security Act: Grants to States for Aid to Families with Dependent Children (AFDC)*, Washington, D.C.: Congressional Research Service, Library of Congress, 24 February 1984, 2.

6. *Congressional Record,* 85th Cong., 2d sess., 1958, 397.

7. Vee Burke, *Brief Legislative History,* 2.

8. Ibid., 3.

9. Committee on Ways and Means, U.S. House of Representatives, *Background Material and Data on Programs within the Jurisdiction of the Committee on Ways and Means,* 21 February 1984, 308.

10. Howard Oberheu, "Time on Assistance," unpublished paper, Office of Research and Statistics, Office of Policy, Social Security Administration, Department of Health and Human Services, 1982.

Part II
Policy Enactment and Implementation

3
Proposed Federal Policy Changes

Government policy toward the poor took a sudden turn under the Reagan administration. Shortly after taking office in January 1981, President Reagan submitted a federal budget that included significant reductions in social programs. Included in this budget were policy changes in AFDC designed to reduce federal spending by removing some families from the welfare rolls and reducing benefits to others. But these changes were more than budget cuts, for they represented a fundamental shift in the philosophy behind the nation's primary welfare program.

To save federal dollars and wean the working poor from "dependency," the administration chose to change AFDC eligibility and benefits in highly technical ways. There were other ways they could have saved money, such as lowering the federal reimbursement rate in each state by a few percentage points. However, they instead chose to alter specific provisions in detail. Because AFDC is a jointly financed federal-state program, these changes also had to affect eligibility in all states regardless of the particular benefit structure existing in each state.

The administration chose to change twenty-seven specific AFDC policies in such a way that fewer people would be eligible for benefits and many of those that were eligible would receive reduced benefits. Of the twenty-seven reform provisions proposed by the Reagan administration in 1981, five were directed at working families. These changes limited eligibility and benefits to those families with earnings who had been eligible for partial AFDC payments. The revisions were highly technical but their effects were quite significant. The new rules reduced the amount of earned income that could be disregarded in determining AFDC benefits. Put simply, mothers would be able to keep less of their earned income before their benefits were cut or, in many cases, eliminated entirely.

The five major policy changes targeted on working AFDC recipients (almost all mothers) are described here because they radically altered the nature and scope of AFDC. The work-incentive provisions had been the subject of controversy for many years. Some policymakers thought the provisions essential and wrestled with ways to increase work incentives without significantly increasing overall program costs. Others believed that while the incentives were sound in principle, they had little positive effect on the labor-force behavior of AFDC recipients. Still others, like those in the Reagan administration, viewed the work-incentive provisions as encouraging welfare dependency. The outcome was a drastic reduction in the work-incentive rules, explained as follows.

The first change was the *establishment of a cap on eligibility*. Any family with income above 150 percent of the state need standard (which varies by state) could not receive AFDC. As mentioned in chapter 2, the need standard is used to determine eligibility for AFDC. It is different from (and always lower than) the poverty threshold; moreover, many states do not pay benefits equal to their need standard. Prior to the policy change, a family with modest earnings and high work-related expenses (such as transportation and child care) might have qualified for AFDC based on low "countable" income (gross earnings minus work expenses). The new rules terminated eligibility for families whose gross income exceeded 150 percent of the state's need standard, regardless of their work expenses.

For example, the need standard for a four-person family in Pennsylvania was $395 in 1980; 150 percent of this put the eligibility ceiling at $592. Families with gross monthly income over this ceiling would now be ineligible for AFDC. Previously some families with income exceeding this amount might still qualify if they had unusually high work expenses.

The second provision was the *limitation of the $30 plus one-third disregard to four months*. Before 1981, families with earnings were allowed to deduct $30 and one-third of the remaining income from their gross wages when calculating their AFDC benefit. Under the new rule, recipients would be able to use this disregard only for four months, which would sharply reduce and in some cases eliminate AFDC benefits to working parents after that period of time.

For example, a four-person family with $350 in earnings would be eligible for $282 in AFDC using the $30 plus one-third deduction, but, four months later, when the disregard expired, the family's AFDC grant would drop to $195. In many cases, the family's grant would drop to zero when the $30 plus one-third disregard expired.

The third provision required the *application of the earned income disregard of $30 plus one-third of the remainder to net income (after childcare and work expense deductions) rather than to gross income*. Before 1981, families with earnings applied the $30 plus one-third reduction to their gross wages when calculating their AFDC benefit. Under the proposed rules, the $30 plus one-third reduction would be taken after child-care and work-expense deductions had been applied. This change reduced the value of the $30 plus one-third disregard, since the disregard would now be applied to a smaller amount of earnings. This in turn reduced payments to working recipients.

The fourth provision called for the *standardization of work expenses at $75 and limitation of child-care expenses at $160 per child per month.* Previously, working recipients could deduct reasonable work-related expenses such as taxes, transportation, and uniforms, as well as child-care costs, from their earnings when their benefits were calculated. The new rule eliminated this flexibility and standardized the work-expense disregard at $75 per month for full-time workers and at $50 for part-time workers. The new rule also capped the child-care disregard at $160 per month for each child.

The fifth provision required the *advance counting of any Earned Income Tax Credit* (EITC). Earners with annual incomes below $10,000 and at least one dependent child are eligible for a refundable tax credit from the IRS. Whereas under previous law the tax credit was considered income only if an AFDC recipient actually received it, the new policy required that the EITC be counted as income in determining AFDC benefits whether or not it was actually received. So in some cases the AFDC recipient's grant would automatically be reduced even though the family had not received the tax credit.

For example, a family earning $350 that was eligible for a monthly tax credit of $40 but that was unaware of the credit or did not know how to apply for it—a common situation—would have its AFDC benefit calculated on the basis of $390 in gross income ($350 in wages plus $40 in EITC), regardless of the fact that the family had only $350 in income. The $40 EITC was counted as income even though the family did not receive it.

It must be remembered that these are only a few of the AFDC policy changes proposed by President Reagan in 1981. Other changes were enacted to restrict eligibility to nonworking families as well (some of these are discussed in chapter 5). In addition, President Reagan proposed budget cuts in food stamps and Medicaid that also promised to reduce benefits to AFDC families.

The Rationale for the Policy Changes

To understand the reasons behind the changes, one must understand the Reagan administration's perspective on public-assistance programs. In their budget documents, administration officials characterized public assistance programs as fraught with problems, stating that:

> Benefits were excessive and poorly targeted.
>   Waste and error were rife, partly as a result of poor program design . . . and partly because of pervasive mismanagement.
>   In some cases, fundamental program designs were so profoundly deficient that even the best management could not overcome the perverse incentives, inequities and needless expenditures that resulted.
>   As a consequence of these problems, literally billions of scarce tax dollars were needlessly wasted.[1]

The administration further stressed that reductions in federal spending were necessary to the economic recovery. Office of Management and Budget Director David Stockman, the primary spokesman for the administration's position on spending cuts, asserted that "elimination of unnecessary federal spending aids the economic recovery program whose success will benefit all low-income Americans."[2]

The view of public assistance programs as bloated shaped the AFDC policy changes in 1981. Since the administration had come into office on a platform of reducing federal spending, the "unnecessary federal spending" in AFDC was a prime target. The administration estimated that its 1981 proposed changes would save $1.2 billion in federal funds. Because AFDC is a federal-state matching program, this was to result in state savings of another $1.2 billion for FY 1982. The new policies were also designed to amend several aspects of AFDC that the administration considered to be a distortion of the program's purposes. The administration believed that AFDC benefits were "poorly targeted" and that many persons received AFDC who were not "truly needy." The proposed eligibility cap of 150 percent of the state need standard sought to eliminate benefits to recipients with the most income even though most of these families were still poor. Yet the eligibility ceiling designed to eliminate the nonneedy welfare recipients was ill-conceived. There may have been AFDC recipients with relatively high incomes in some states, but a cap based on the state need standard is not the best means for eliminating grants to these recipients. Since need standards vary from state to state, a 150 percent cap might target a family with $800 in monthly income as nonneedy in some states, but it would also eliminate benefits for a family with $450 in monthly income in South Carolina and a family with $350 in Alabama. The 150 percent cap eliminated benefits for many families well below the poverty line.

Administration officials also believed that the highly touted work-incentive provisions were in fact "dependency incentives" and encouraged AFDC mothers to retain some tie to the welfare system. Thus, by limiting the $30 plus one-third disregard to four months, the administration believed it was providing the incentive needed to make the transition from welfare to self-support. Yet policymakers must try to reward work effort. The supplemental AFDC benefits provided under the work-incentive provisions prior to 1981 ensured that working women had more disposable income than did nonworking recipients. The AFDC work-incentive provisions ensured that work was rewarded, a policy direction that should be maintained.

Though the administration pledged itself to maintaining the "social safety net" to protect the "truly needy," it clearly believed that most working women did not fit into this category. That these families had earnings was seen by the administration as evidence of their ability to support themselves fully through work. As chapter 8 will show, this reflects a lack of basic understanding about AFDC and the families receiving it.

Moreover, the administration failed to offer any new assistance to the "working poor"—including those families who had lost AFDC benefits under the proposed rules. While policymakers have often debated the effectiveness of AFDC work incentives, none have challenged the needs of low-income workers and their families. The administration proposals eliminated the AFDC supplement that many of these families received but did not offer any new means of assisting them. This is troubling in part because working-poor families exhibit the very self-supporting behavior that the administration hoped to foster.

These deficiencies in the administration's rationale were apparently overlooked because of the haste with which it developed its budget cuts. The provisions were not reviewed by staff of the Department of Health and Human Services (HHS), as is normal practice. In the past when AFDC policy changes had been proposed, the Office of Family Assistance and the Office of the Assistant Secretary for Planning and Evaluation, within HHS, would assess their likely impact. Such reviews documented who would be helped by the changes, who would suffer reduced benefits, and by how much. In 1981, however, the AFDC proposals were developed by a longtime Reagan aide, Robert Carlson, then Special Assistant to the President. Neither HHS, as the executive agency in charge of AFDC, nor the Office of Management and Budget (OMB) carefully studied the proposals. Consequently, the proposals were included in the president's budget package without an analysis of their likely impact. As one major newspaper noted, "Stockman didn't get all the facts together before he began slashing."[3]

Initial Responses to the Administration Proposals

Upon release of the AFDC budget proposals in 1981, private research organizations compiled reports that pointed out several defects. The first such report, conducted by the Center for the Study of Social Policy and published in March 1981, examined the effects of the proposed policy changes on AFDC recipients in each state.[4] This analysis yielded two important findings. First, the AFDC cuts, when combined with other related program cuts affecting the poor, promised to push families deeper into poverty. In order to examine the likely effects of the AFDC policy changes, it became evident that one must also consider related programs like food stamps and Medicaid, since all AFDC families are also eligible for these. Food stamp benefits are inversely related to AFDC grants; that is, if a family's grant is diminished, the amount of food stamps will increase, although not by enough to make up for the entire AFDC loss. Also, as mentioned earlier, all families who receive AFDC are automatically covered by Medicaid. Conversely, many families who lose AFDC also lose Medicaid. The center calculated a typical family's AFDC grant under both existing and proposed rules. Use of state-by-state data was necessary to show the differential impact of the proposals among states— a step the administration apparently ignored.

The report illustrated the combined effects of the policy changes on AFDC families' disposable income, excluding the value of Medicaid, in each state. Total monthly disposable income, including earnings, AFDC, food stamps, and energy assistance, was calculated as a percentage of the poverty threshold under both current and proposed guidelines.

Table 3–1 shows the decrease in total monthly disposable income as a percentage of the poverty threshold for working AFDC families in 47 states plus the District of Columbia. The table demonstrates that total monthly disposable income was reduced in all states, bringing many families below the poverty line. In those states in which the average earnings are highest, families lost the most. In New York and California, for example, where payment levels and average earnings are higher than in most states, average family income among working families would drop from 119 and 129 percent of the poverty line, respectively, to 89 and 91 percent. Although the proposed cuts did not drop as dramatically in low-payment states, their effects on families in these states were shown to be even more devastating since these families had incomes far below the official poverty standard even before the cuts. Overall, the average family

Table 3–1
The Effect of the Budget Reconciliation Act on Monthly Disposable Income[a] and Poverty Status[b] of AFDC Working Families

	Existing Law 1981		Under Proposed Cuts	
	Disposable Income ($)	Percent of Poverty	Disposable Income ($)	Percent of Poverty
Alabama	$406	69%	$365	62%
Arizona	449	76	374	63
Arkansas	464	79	454	77
California	758	129	537	91
Colorado	601	102	477	81
Connecticut	731	124	534	91
Delaware	589	100	480	82
District of Columbia	616	104	499	85
Florida	491	83	402	68
Georgia	453	77	368	62
Idaho	634	108	512	87
Illinois	590	100	459	78
Indiana	564	96	463	79
Iowa	664	113	501	85
Kansas	612	104	478	81
Kentucky	522	89	470	80
Louisiana	449	76	371	63
Maine	649	110	526	89
Maryland	590	100	485	82
Massachusetts	685	116	511	87
Michigan	675	114	532	90
Minnesota	742	126	537	91
Mississippi	504	85	442	75
Missouri	570	97	483	82
Montana	566	96	478	81
Nebraska	656	111	498	85
New Hampshire	649	110	515	87
New Jersey	661	112	497	84
New Mexico	546	93	439	75

Table 3–1continued

Table 3–1 *continued*

	Existing Law 1981		Under Proposed Cuts	
	Disposable Income ($)	Percent of Poverty	Disposable Income ($)	Percent of Poverty
New York	703	119	525	89
North Carolina	504	86	441	75
North Dakota	684	116	521	88
Ohio	543	92	430	73
Oklahoma	587	100	468	79
Oregon	628	107	496	84
Pennsylvania	631	107	501	85
Rhode Island	720	122	567	96
South Carolina	495	84	453	77
South Dakota	633	107	489	83
Tennessee	456	77	438	74
Texas	409	69	372	63
Utah	629	107	511	87
Vermont	768	130	543	92
Virginia	549	93	439	75
Washington	713	121	545	93
West Virginia	493	84	404	69
Wisconsin	750	127	537	91
Wyoming	593	101	479	81
Average	$595	101%	$476	81%

Source: "Profiles of Families in Poverty: Effects of the FY 1983 Budget Proposals on the Poor," Center for the Study of Social Policy, 25 February 1982.

Note: Alaska, Hawaii, and Nevada are not included because of small sample sizes.

[a] Disposable income figures for each state represent the sum of monthly earnings plus AFDC, food stamps, and energy assistance benefits for a working AFDC family of three, assuming average earnings for AFDC families in that state.

[b] Poverty status is expressed in terms of monthly disposable income divided by the federally established 1981 poverty level for a family of three, or $589 per month.

income would decline from 101 to 81 percent of the poverty standard nationwide.

The study also found that the cost savings resulting from AFDC reductions would be partially offset by an increase in food stamp benefits. The administration had failed to account for this effect on food stamp outlays in its estimate of cost savings. Moreover, since food stamp benefits are financed fully by the federal government and AFDC is financed jointly by the federal and state governments, the shift from AFDC to food stamp expenditures actually transferred a portion of the costs from the states to the federal government.

It was discovered that the proposed AFDC regulations also created a significant work disincentive. The changes would reduce a working family's income almost to the level of a nonworking family's income. Thus, the administration's proposals would virtually eliminate any financial incentive for AFDC mothers to work. The incomes of working AFDC families would be reduced so much under the new proposals that working parents in many states would be little better off—and sometimes worse off—than AFDC mothers who did not work.

Table 3–2 shows that in twelve states the 1981 proposals would in fact push the disposable incomes of working families below those of nonworking families. For example, under the proposed cuts in California, a working mother with two children would have $537 in disposable income while a nonworking mother would have $584, or $47 more in disposable income. Before the 1981 changes, a working mother would have had $758 in disposable income, or $174 more than the nonworking mother with $584. In all cases, the administration's proposals reduced the differential between working and nonworking mothers.

Put another way, the proposed rules dramatically increased the "marginal tax rate"—the rate at which benefits are reduced as earnings rise. Each additional dollar earned after four months on the job would result in a net income gain of only one cent. Ninety-nine cents would be "taxed away" through reductions in AFDC and food stamp benefits. In some states, working mothers would end up with a net income loss if they earned more money. For example, working mothers in the state of Washington earning $525 a month would end up 30 cents worse off for each additional dollar they earned. In short, when the proposals were carefully scrutinized, they were found to penalize work effort by discouraging those who were working from working harder and increasing their earnings, as well as by discouraging those not already working from getting a job.

Table 3–2
The Effect of Employment on the Monthly Disposable Income[a] of AFDC Families: Comparison of FY 1981, and FY 1982

| | FY 1981 Prior to Budget Reconciliation Act | | | Under Proposed Cuts (FY 1982) | | |
| | Disposable Income | | | Disposable Income | | |
	Nonworking Parent	Working Parent	Difference[b]	Nonworking Parent	Working Parent	Difference[b]
Alabama	$307	$406	$ 99	$307	$365	$ 59
Arizona	370	449	79	370	374	4
Arkansas	311	464	154	311	454	144
California	584	758	174	584	537	−47
Colorado	468	601	133	468	477	9
Connecticut	563	731	168	563	534	−29
Delaware	438	589	151	438	480	42
District of Columbia	450	616	166	450	499	49
Florida	377	491	114	377	402	25
Georgia	362	453	91	362	368	6
Idaho	466	634	168	466	512	46
Illinois	449	590	141	449	459	10
Indiana	419	564	144	419	463	44
Iowa	505	664	159	505	501	−4
Kansas	467	612	145	467	478	10
Kentucky	376	522	147	376	470	94
Louisiana	366	449	83	366	371	5
Maine	462	649	187	462	526	64
Maryland	432	590	158	432	485	54
Massachusetts	518	685	167	518	511	−6
Michigan	513	675	162	513	532	19
Minnesota	573	742	169	573	537	−36
Mississippi	287	504	216	287	442	154
Missouri	409	570	161	409	483	74
Montana	472	566	94	472	478	6
Nebraska	500	656	156	500	498	−2

New Hampshire	505	649	145	505	515	10
New Jersey	500	661	162	500	497	−3
New Mexico	417	546	129	417	439	22
New York	537	703	166	537	525	−12
North Carolina	369	504	135	369	441	72
North Dakota	525	684	159	525	521	−4
Ohio	422	543	121	422	430	8
Oklahoma	434	587	152	434	468	34
Oregon	462	628	166	462	496	33
Pennsylvania	465	631	166	465	501	36
Rhode Island	567	720	152	567	567	0
South Carolina	334	495	161	334	453	119
South Dakota	478	633	155	478	489	12
Tennessee	322	456	134	322	438	116
Texas	306	409	104	306	372	66
Utah	503	629	126	503	511	9
Vermont	596	768	172	596	543	−53
Virginia	417	549	132	417	439	22
Washington	551	713	161	551	545	−6
West Virginia	380	493	112	380	404	24
Wisconsin	579	750	171	579	537	−42
Wyoming	471	593	122	471	479	8
U.S. Average	$450	$595	$146	$450	$476	$ 26

Source: "Profiles of Families in Poverty: Effects of the FY 1983 Budget Proposals on the Poor," Center for the Study of Social Policy, 25 February 1982.

Note: Alaska, Hawaii, & Nevada are not included because of small sample sizes.

[a] Disposable income figures shown for each state represent the sum of earnings, AFDC, Food Stamps, EITC, and energy assistance benefits for either a working or non-working family in that state. Earnings are calculated based on the average earnings for an AFDC family in that state.

[b] All numbers do not add due to rounding.

The press began to focus on the work-disincentive issue, and several major newspapers and journals printed editorials decrying the policy changes. The *New York Times* commented:

> Everyone gains when the working poor are allowed to keep some public assistance as an incentive to work. The poor workers gain: they end up with more income than if wholly dependent on welfare. Government gains: every dollar earned means 60 cents saved in benefits. The work ethic gains: the labor performed yields pride and productivity. The Administration is enthusiastic about incentives elsewhere, but not for the working poor.[5]

The *Washington Post* stated:

> What about the families that try to help themselves by working? Back in the "old days" of welfare debate, it was thought that people who took the sort of ill-paid, periodic jobs that are the welfare recipient's normal lot should keep at least a third—and preferably more—of their earnings for their efforts. In the Reagan scheme, however, the question is not how much better off working recipients should be but how much worse off.[6]

The *Boston Globe* similarly noted:

> Liberals, who for years have been seeking changes that would expand benefits, know the difficulties of changing welfare policies. Now the Reagan team may understand that they face similar hurdles in trying to reduce benefits. If the gap between the disposable income derived from work and that derived from welfare is reduced to little or nothing, the rational decision by the working poor will be to quit work. The safety net will soon become filled. That would be an ironic result from changes made by an Administration seeking to instill the work ethic.[7]

Several members of Congress also noted publicly their dismay at the AFDC work-disincentive discovery. As Representative Les Aspin (D–Wisconsin) told the *New York Times,* "The one thing I think everybody can agree [on] is that there isn't enough work incentive now, and to make it less is crazy."[8]

Asked about these findings in 1981, a spokesman for the Office of Management and Budget acknowledged that the administration's proposals would penalize low-paid working families on AFDC but termed the penalty "modest," denying that it was a major change in the work incentive. At the same time, he admitted that the administration had not done a state-by-state analysis of the potential impact of the policy changes on individual families. A few days later, David Stockman asserted on a television program that working AFDC parents would be penalized only in "isolated cases." However, Edwin Dale, OMB's official spokesman, conceded one week later that the work disincentive was broader than Stockman's comments implied and that the proposed cuts would worsen the work-disincentive problem that already existed in AFDC.

As the *Chicago Sun-Times* noted in its editorial entitled "Hasty Budget Cuts,"

> It's all fresh evidence that the Reagan team failed to do its homework in some areas. A spokesman for the Office of Management and Budget admitted—with a red face, we hope—there had been no state-by-state analysis of how the Reagan cuts might hit families.[9]

In reply to a reporter's question about what would happen if the poor quit their jobs on account of the work-disincentive features, a White House official dismissed the problem by saying that such families would then be required to "work off" their benefits under a "workfare" program.[10] Under the administration's workfare proposal, welfare recipients would be mandated to work off their benefits in part-time positions with government or nonprofit agencies. The number of hours of work required is calculated by dividing the AFDC benefit by $3.35, the minimum wage. For example, a nonworking mother receiving $60 per week in AFDC would be required to work eighteen hours per week in a newly created job that would benefit the community ($60 divided by $3.35/hour = eighteen hours).

The administration's use of workfare as an answer to the work-disincentive feature of its policy changes was entirely inadequate. The policy changes were justified by the contention that people who quit their jobs because they now could get just as much money by staying home would have to participate in workfare anyway. But administration officials failed to see the very real difference between workfare jobs, which pay no wages, and private sector wage-paying jobs, which these mothers already had.

As the British weekly the *Economist* commented,

> Many welfare reformers have stubbed their toes on the hard problem of reconciling incentives to work with justice to the neediest. The administration has an answer of sorts; it is called workfare, was tried out in California with little noticeable success when Mr. Reagan was governor and calls for poor mothers with no children under two to contribute 20 hours of work a week to the community. This work will be hard for communities to organize and is unlikely to prepare poor women for the world of real work.[11]

One year after proposing the 1981 AFDC policy changes, the administration put forth another rationale for its AFDC cuts. OMB asserted that the 1981 changes (as well as new proposals to further curtail benefits in 1982) were intended to solve the so-called notch problem that allowed working AFDC families to have more money than working families not on AFDC. The work-incentive provisions allowed small supplemental payments to be made to families with low wages. This inevitably meant that families who had the same wages but who were not eligible for AFDC (either because of family composition or because they did not meet the assets test) would have less disposable income. This has been a characteristic of AFDC since the work-incentive features were established.

The Reagan administration claimed that its policy changes solved the problem of unequal treatment of people in similar circumstances.[12] Allowing working AFDC families to have greater disposable income than working families not on welfare was an inequitable situation, according to the administration, that was unfair to families supported by earnings alone. The administration asserted that its policy changes would resolve the inequity by terminating AFDC grants to the working poor. This way, all working-poor families would be treated the same: none would receive assistance, and none would be better off than a neighbor earning the same amount.

This expost facto rationale for the administration's policy changes was not entirely convincing. The administration's response to a troubling inequity was simply to cut benefits for those who were slightly better off. This reasoning fails to acknowledge that the working AFDC family and the non-AFDC family earning the same wages are both poor. Simply to discard assistance to one group is an inadequate policy response to a real need for cash assistance by both families. True, the inequity dissolves, but both are now in the same inadequate position: two groups are living in poverty instead of just one. To claim that its policy changes solved the inequity problem in AFDC may be literally true, but it was a harsh solution that failed to help either family.

In summary, the administration's AFDC proposals appeared to have been hastily developed, with little scrutiny of how they were likely to affect recipients. Moreover, the proposals represented a radical departure from existing policy and philosophy. For the first time, federal policy was based on the belief that work incentives actually encouraged dependency. Liberals and conservatives have always viewed the work-incentive provisions as encouraging work and discouraging dependency. The Reagan administration ignored the work-encouragement aspect and believed that the provisions encouraged dependency. Yet it did nothing to replace the work-incentive feature and in effect left out an important half of the work-welfare equation. In the final analysis, the administration's policy proposals left the working poor to fend for themselves, a drastic reversal of prior public policy.

Notes

1. *Major Themes and Additional Budget Details, Fiscal Year 1984,* Office of Management and Budget, Washington, D.C., 27.

2. Ibid.

3. "Don't Slaughter the Budget," *Chicago Sun-Times,* 16 April 1981, 29.

4. *The Poor: Profiles of Families in Poverty,* Center for the Study of Social Policy, 27 March 1981; and *Profiles of Families in Poverty: Effects of the FY 1982 and 1983 Budget Proposals on the Poor,* Idem., 25 February 1982.

5. "Sob Sisters," *New York Times,* 3 March 1982. Copyright 1982 by the New York Times Company. Reprinted by permission.

6. "What's Happened to Welfare?" *Washington Post,* 2 March 1982.

7. "The Welfare Tightrope," *Boston Globe,* 23 March 1981, 14. Reprinted by courtesy of the *Boston Globe.*

8. *New York Times,* 29 March 1981, 22. Copyright 1981 by the New York Times Company. Reprinted by permission.

9. "Hasty Budget Cuts," *Chicago Sun-Times,* 23 March 1981, 31. Copyright News Group Chicago, Inc., 1981. Reprinted with permission of the *Chicago Sun-Times.*

10. Linda Demkovich, "Reagan's Welfare Cuts Could Force Many Working Poor Back on the Dole," *National Journal* (January 2, 1982):22.

11. *Economist,* 10 April 1981, 26. Reprinted with permission.

12. "Reforming Entitlement Programs," *Major Themes and Additional Budget Details: FY 1983,* Executive Office of the President, Office of Management and Budget, 38

4
The Omnibus Budget Reconciliation Act of 1981

Betwen the time Ronald Reagan was elected president in November 1980 and the time he submitted his first budget to Congress in February 1981, adminsitration officials devised AFDC policy changes outlined in the previous chapter. Clearly, there was not a great deal of time to assess the likely effects of the proposals, considering that transition teams were in charge and a whole new government was being assembled. Moreover, the AFDC policy changes were but a few among hundreds of specific budget reductions.

Yet these hastily devised changes were enacted almost in their entirety by Congress. Considering the serious questions raised about the work-disincentive feature of the AFDC proposals, it is surprising that the proposals made their way through the congressional gauntlet with few alterations. The explanation of how this occurred lies in the administration's successful dominance of the congressional budget reconciliation procedures—technical procedures that are often overlooked in legislative analyses but that played a key role in the president's legislative victory in 1981.

The 97th Congress, convened in January 1981, followed budget procedures that had been established in 1974. It was the unique use of these established budget procedures in 1981, the economic crisis at the time, and President Reagan's popularity that allowed the president's proposals to be enacted in whole. The 1974 procedures were employed in 1981 in a manner that bypassed traditional interest-group politics and precluded full congressional debate of specific provisions. In addition, the 1981 budget process fueled an intense debate on the viability of the budget procedures. As such, it is useful to explore briefly the budget procedure itself before describing how it was utilized in 1981.

The Congressional Budget Process

Prior to the Budget Control and Impoundment Act of 1974, critical policy decisions were made in an uncoordinated fashion by congressional committees, each of which had its own assigned jurisdictions. For instance, the House Ways and Means Committee and the Senate Finance Committee each was responsible for AFDC legislation. In addition to these "policy" committees, the Appropriations Committee in each chamber appropriated or spent the amount of money necessary to fund individual programs. Under this committee process, spending was the product of numerous isolated decisions made throughout the year, making it difficult, if not impossible, to determine overall priorities or to gauge the net effect of spending decisions. Legislators did not relate their individual decisions to total budget surpluses or deficits or to assessments of current economic conditions. In short, they did not consolidate their decisions into a coherent fiscal policy.

Congress passed the Budget Control and Impoundment Act to impose fiscal discipline on itself and to restore order to the chaotic budgetary process. Congress wanted to establish procedures that would force it to make spending decisions more responsibly. At the same time, Congress hoped to use the act to set priorities among the various federal spending programs. It also hoped to better control presidential spending authority in the wake of skepticism arising from, for example, the Vietnam War, Nixon's impoundment of funds, and Watergate.

The 1974 act required Congress to determine fiscal policy goals each spring through a tentative spending resolution that would guide revenue and spending measures until a final and binding second resolution was passed each fall. A process of "reconciling" committee actions with the second budget resolution was established. The act also created a new budget committee in each chamber and gave it the responsibility for formulating congressional guidelines with respect to fiscal policy and spending priorities.

In 1981, President Reagan's budget director, David Stockman (a former congressman from Michigan), used his detailed knowledge of the budget process to achieve both the policy changes and the spending cuts sought by the administration. Stockman knew that whereas he had a good chance of forging a coalition of conservatives on the House floor, he had little chance of getting the individual House policy committees to go along with the administration's proposals. He also knew that there was enormous pressure to cut federal spending in light of rising inflation, a coming recession, and a mounting federal deficit. Because of these unique circumstances, Stockman was able to use the budget procedures in a way that had happened only once before, in 1980.

The Stage Is Set

The first step in the budget process was to pass a first concurrent budget resolution in the spring that set tentative spending targets for the coming fiscal year. On February 18, 1981, the administration sent to Congress an outline of its budget entitled "The President's Program for Economic Recovery," containing substantial spending reductions in social programs. Three weeks later, on March 10, the administration sent to Congress its formal revision of the budget originally submitted by former President Carter. This budget contained even more spending cuts than the "Program for Economic Recovery" document. Stockman maintained that the second round of cuts was necessary to reduce the federal deficit, which was worse than he had originally thought. The revised budget called for $37 billion in spending cuts.

The Senate Budget Committee acted quickly to produce a first budget resolution that virtually mirrored the president's request. This was passed by the entire Senate within one month. In the House, however, there was more dissension.

The House Budget Committee put together a budget resolution that would save $15.8 billion, far short of the $37 billion in spending cuts sought by the administration, which immediately denounced the plan as inadequate. As a result, conservative Democrat Phillip Gramm from Texas and Republican Delbert Latta from Ohio offered a substitute amendment to the Budget Committee's resolution. On May 7, 1981, the substitute amendment, instead of the House Budget Committee resolution, passed the House by a vote of 253 to 176. Called "Gramm–Latta I," the substitute contained almost all the president's spending cuts, calling for $36.6 billion in savings. Not only did the substitute call for far greater savings than did the resolution fashioned by the House Budget Committee, but for the first time since the 1974 act had established these procedures, nonentitlement savings were included. Ordinarily, the budget resolution dealt only with savings in entitlement programs, and nonentitlement or discretionary programs were left to the appropriations committees. However, in 1981, Gramm–Latta I included savings in discretionary programs as well. This is why Gramm–Latta I called for such greater savings than did the Budget Committee's resolution, which contained only entitlement-program savings as intended in the 1974 act.

A conference committee between the House and Senate reached agreement on areas where the two resolutions differed and yielded a first concurrent budget resolution calling for $35.1 billion in savings. AFDC savings were to total $1.2 billion, based on estimates of how much the administration's twenty-seven policy proposals would save. The conference report was agreed to on May 20, 1981.

Reconciliation

The first concurrent resolution called for savings to be accomplished through a "reconciliation bill." The resolution contained reconciliation instructions to each of the policy committees in the House and Senate, giving each a deadline by which it was to achieve a predetermined amount of savings. The committees were then required to report out legislation that would achieve the amount of savings called for. The fifteen House committees had less than three weeks to report out the $35.1 billion in savings.

The reconciliation instructions did not require that the committees produce the exact same spending cuts as those identified in the budget resolution—just that they yield the same amount of money. The committees then were to submit their draft legislation to the Budget Committee, where the pieces would be packaged into a single reconciliation bill.

The 1974 budget act called for reconciliation procedures to bring spending bills crafted by committees in line with the budget resolution. It was at this stage that the process was used differently in 1981 and allowed all of President Reagan's proposals to be enacted in one sweeping bill.

The fourteen Senate committees reported out their bills to the Senate Budget Committee, and, as expected, achieved the first resolution's target of $35 billion in cuts. The fifteen House committees reported out bills that, when packaged together in a reconciliation bill, totaled $37.5 billion in savings, surpassing the reconciliation directives by $2.4 billion.

Included in the House reconciliation package was an AFDC bill that would have saved $669 million instead of the $1.2 billion included in the first concurrent budget resolution. The House Ways and Means Committee (1) rejected the administration's cap at 150 percent of the state need standard, (2) would have expanded the $30 plus one-third disregard to $50 and one-third, (3) would have allowed a $50 plus one-third disregard for twelve months instead of four months, and (4) made some other minor changes to make the earned income cuts less harsh. The committee was able to make fewer cuts in AFDC than the first resolution called for by making larger cuts in other programs within their jurisdiction. That way, it avoided some of the harshest AFDC cuts while still making substantial cuts in the program and making up for others with cuts in other programs.

All of the budgets that were developed were based on extremely shaky economic forecasts and were so technical that they were all but impossible to understand. In his sketch of David Stockman in the *Atlantic,* William Greider reported the following:

> The budget politics of 1981, which produced such clear and dramatic rhetoric from both sides, was, in fact, based upon a bewildering set of numbers that confused even those, like Stockman, who produced them.

"None of us really understands what's going on with all these numbers," Stockman confessed at one point. "You've got so many different budgets out and so many different baselines and such complexity now in the interactive parts of the budget between policy action and the economic environment and all the internal mysteries of the budget, and there are a lot of them. People are getting from A to B and it's not clear how they are getting there. It's not clear how we got there, and it's not clear how [House Budget Committee Chairman] Jones is going to get there."[1]

The Senate, with a Republican majority, passed its reconciliation bill without fanfare on June 25, 1981. In the House, however, a fierce struggle began as soon as the bill took form. Jim Jones, chairman of the House Budget Committee, fashioned a bill out of the committee reports which, while too austere for many liberals, excluded many of the harshest cuts in entitlement programs. Jones knew that the House conservatives would attempt to substitute their own plan for his, but he thought he would have enough votes to win passage of his bill.

The real fight concerned the rule under which the reconciliation bill was to come to a vote. Because the House Rules Committee was controlled by moderate Democrats, the committee voted for a rule that would have forced the Republican alternative to be voted on in six separate votes. In other words, the Republican proposal was to be divided into six pieces. Democrats reasoned that this way they would have a better chance of defeating the individual proposals and passing their own version.

However, the blow came on June 25, 1981, when the whole House convened to act on the reconciliation bill. President Reagan had lobbied conservative Democrats to vote against the rule as passed by the Rules Committee. Republicans prevailed, with the help of conservative Democrats. The rule was rejected by a vote of 217 to 210 and a substitution rule was adopted instead that allowed only one or two amendments to the Republican proposal. This meant that the Republican proposal, no longer divided into six separate pieces, was to be voted on in a single up or down motion—exactly what Stockman had hoped for from the beginning. The administration felt it could achieve all of its budget cuts if it could force a single vote because many members were afraid to go on record as having voted against President Reagan, who enjoyed so much public popularity.

The House was to vote on the Omnibus Budget Reconciliation Act on June 26, 1981, just before adjourning for the Fourth of July holiday. Known as Gramm–Latta II, the Republican proposal had been drafted by OMB and conservative members of Congress. Liberals and moderates were furious because the Gramm–Latta II substitute had not been made available to House members before the floor vote. Members finally received copies of the document—which was several inches thick—while on the floor, but had difficulty tracking its provisions since there were no page numbers and no index. There was not enough time for members to read all the changes, let alone to determine their impact or compare them to current law.

Liberal and moderate members immediately voiced their frustrations on the floor. They had just lost their rule on account of President Reagan's persuasiveness, and now they were faced with an alternative that they feared contained harsher cuts than their own carefully crafted reconciliation package. Moreover, they didn't even know what was in Gramm–Latta II. Speaker of the House Tip O'Neill stated:

> Mr. Chairman, there is no doubt that there is utter confusion. And why should there not be? Copies of the amendment are now available for the first time, and most of the Members have not even seen the bill. The truth of the matter is, the front page of the *[Washington] Star* today says that the author of the bill has not seen it himself.[2]

Most distressing for many members was the abuse of the legislative process that was involved in Gramm–Latta II. The action had taken place so quickly that they realized they were being tied to the first budget resolution's spending cuts instead of being allowed to revise these with a second budget resolution. Congressman Ted Weiss (D–New York) summed up the feelings of many in his statement before the floor vote:

> Mr. Chairman, the Reagan Omnibus Reconciliation Amendments Act that we are debating today represents the culmination of a process that has gone totally out of control. For only the second time since the passage of the Budget Control and Impoundment Act of 1974, the process of reconciliation is being used in conjunction with the first budget resolution. This drastically changes the nature of the budget process, making the first resolution's spending figures into mandatory spending ceilings, instead of the targets or guidelines intended by the authors of the act.[3]

Moreover, several members were disturbed because the Gramm–Latta II substitute had completely bypassed the authorizing committees. By so boldly offering an entire spending package that included entitlement and nonentitlement savings in one amendment, the authorizing committees had had no opportunity to review the proposed cuts. Congressman David Obey (D–Wisconsin) observed:

> The process required by Gramm–Latta is outrageous. We have at least

run the majority proposals through the safety valve of the committee system, whereas with the minority proposals we have run them through no safety valve.[4]

Congressman Ronald Dellums (D–California) expressed frustration at the major structural changes made in programs through what was essentially a budget bill:

> The reconciliation process itself is an extremely dangerous one because we are not simply here talking about budgetary parameters. We are actually repealing law. We are rewriting legislation without ever engaging in the formal procedures of the legislative process. I would suggest we reject this process and go back to the responsibilities that we have to protect the rights of the American people.[5]

Despite these and other objections, the Gramm–Latta II substitute was voted on and passed late in the day of June 26. The amendment passed with the help of conservative Southern Democrats (known as Boll Weevils) by a vote of 217 to 211. Jones and his colleagues were stunned. That single vote was to have historic consequences. For AFDC, Gramm–Latta II included all of the president's original twenty-seven policy changes.

The final Omnibus Budget Reconciliation Act of 1981 was developed out of a House–Senate conference used to iron out differences between the two houses on a particular bill. Because the House and Senate bills were so massive, each containing thousands of specific spending cuts, there were inevitably hundreds of areas in which the House and Senate versions differed. As a result, the conference was actually comprised of fifty-eight subconferences involving some 250 senators and representatives. Agreement was reached with amazing speed. The final bill, according to Robert Reischauer, "had 27 titles and more than 600 pages of legislative language and was fully understood by few, if any, of those voting on it."[6] The result, P.L. 97-35, was enacted on July 31, 1981.

Clearly, the budget process itself was a critical factor in the enactment of President Reagan's first-year policy changes. Because Congress had to vote on an entire spending package in a single vote, because decisions had to be made quickly to accommodate abbreviated schedules, and because authorizing committees had no say in the decision making, the normal congressional budget process that allows constituencies to be heard was eclipsed. In short, "reconciliation provided the mechanism for bypassing normal congressional methods of operation."[7]

Bypassing constituencies was a strategy adopted by David Stockman to prevent outcries of alarm that might obstruct his quest for spending reductions. Yet even he admitted in hindsight that the effect was greatest on those least organized and least vocal, that is, the poor. When he was fashioning the cuts, Stockman tried to maintain an appearance of even-handedness:

> I've got to take something out of Boeing's hide to make this look right . . . if we're ever caught not cutting [trade subsidies to big corporations] while we're biting deeply into the social programs, we're going to have big problems.[8]

Yet it was the poor who bore a disproportionate share of the budget cuts in the end. Concessions were made to the powerful but not to the voiceless poor. As William Greider noted,

> The power flowed to the handful of representatives who could reverse the majority, regardless of the interests they represented. Once the Reagan tacticians began making concessions beyond their "policy-based" agenda, it developed that their trades and compromises and giveaways were utterly indistinguishable from the decades of interest-group accommodations that had preceded them, which they so righteously denounced. What was new about the Reagan revolution, in which oil-royalty owners win and welfare mothers lose? Was the new philosophy so different from old Republicanism when the federal subsidies for Boeing and Westinghouse and General Electric were protected, while federal subsidies for unemployed black teenagers were "zeroed out"? One could go on, at great length, searching for balance and equity in the outcome of the Reagan program. . . . For now, Stockman would concede this much: that "weak clients" suffered for their weakness. "Power is contingent," he said. "The power of these client groups turned out to be stronger than I realized. The client groups know how to make themselves heard. The problem is, unorganized groups can't play in this game."[9]

In looking back on the 1981 budget process, many agree that the process somehow went wrong. Democrats were unable to control a process that they themselves had set in motion when they enacted the budget procedures in 1974. The implications for Congress as a viable institution were enormous, and the debate about the role of the committee system versus the House as a whole was fueled.

The AFDC changes included in OBRA were part of a budget package that was unprecedented both in its level of spending cuts and in its lack of attention to particular provisions. As a result, the budgets of many social program were slashed, reducing benefits and protections to the most vulnerable and least powerful groups in society. AFDC was one such program. All of the administration's twenty-seven provisions were passed exactly as they had been proposed except that the Senate had made the administration's workfare plan optional to states instead of mandatory. Other than this, the administration's AFDC package was adopted in its entirety and triggered a series of intergovernmental activities that are the subject of the next chapter.

Notes

1. William Greider, "The Education of David Stockman," *Atlantic* December 1981:116. Reprinted with permission of the author.

2. *The Congressional Record,* 26 June 1981, H3747.

3. Ibid., H3843.

4. Ibid., H3812.

5. Ibid., H3845.

6. Robert Reischauer, "The Congressional Budget Process," *Federal Budget Policy in the 1980's,* ed. Gregory B. Mills and John L. Palmer (Washington, D.C.: Urban Institute Press, 1984), 389.

7. Ibid., 389.

8. Greider, *Education,* 112–13. Reprinted with permission of the author.

9. Greider, *Education,* 125–26. Reprinted with permission of the author.

5
Implementation at the State Level

Political folklore perpetuates the notion that all policy begins and ends in Washington, D.C. Federal officials tend to believe that their decrees are "the law of the land" and are implemented uniformly across the country. These officials often ignore the several layers and branches of government that are necessarily involved in the implementation of federal laws. This is especially true for AFDC, which is a joint federal-state program with much state and local latitude for policymaking and administration.

Passage of OBRA was only the beginning of a long journey. As soon as the law was enacted and signed by President Reagan, wheels began turning at the federal, state, and local levels of government to carry out the new legislation. The new rules had to be translated into operation. New benefit and eligibility formulas had to be developed and staff needed to be trained in their use. And all of this had to be done in a very short period of time.

Because OBRA became law in August 1981 and was to take effect on October 1, 1981, there was very little time to make the system-wide changes required to carry out the new AFDC provisions. The federal Department of Health and Human Services had to issue regulations quickly for the new law. States had to develop new procedures in August and September 1981. Most states did not have time to wait for HHS to issue regulations and, instead, had to rely on the cryptic legislative language to guide their actions. At the local levels, caseworkers had to recalculate grants using new formulas, and many worked overtime for weeks to meet the implementation timetable. In short, the initial implementation process was carried out with haste at all levels of government.

As noted in chapter 4, the passage of OBRA was largely driven by the budget process in the U.S. Congress, without traditional public hearings and involvement of states and localities and even without the participation of congressional authorizing committees. This caused federal officials to ignore administrative details during enactment of the law. Little attention was given to the necessity of translating the new policies into action at the state and local levels of government.

Insofar as states were considered at all, federal policymakers seem to have viewed them as provinces rather than as political entities in their own right, governed by elected officials. Moreover, thousands of counties, again with their own elected officials and administrative units, had to carry out the new policies.

Given the absence of a direct link between federal legislation and AFDC clients, implementation of the federal AFDC changes was not carried out in a clear and precise manner. Instead, a convoluted web of intergovernmental relationships and activities was involved. The elements of this intergovernmental system are depicted in figure 5–1, and a brief description of them follows to illustrate the many points at which federal AFDC policies are further shaped before they actually reach the client.

At the federal level, the Office of Management and Budget initiated, and Congress passed, the new provisions of the law. The Office of Family Assistance, part of the Social Security Administration within the Department of Health and Human Services, drafted and published the regulations for the new law. The ball was then passed to state legislatures, which created or altered state AFDC legislation—in some cases, bringing it into compliance with the new federal law, and in other cases, making changes independent of the OBRA policies. The state departments of public welfare, as the agencies administering AFDC, rewrote administrative regulations to guide implementation of the new provisions. In many instances, state administrators would send out a set of guidelines one week and another set undoing the first one the following week because a new interpretation of the rules had been made. State administrators typically sent local offices dozens of memos and instruction manuals spelling out how the new federal rules were to be implemented in that state.

In several states, governor's offices and budget bureaus became involved in order to project cost savings and expenditures for the annual state budgets. State and federal district courts also played an important role in shaping the implementation of the new provisions because numerous suits were brought over states' interpretations of the federal law.

At the local level, county and city welfare agencies translated the policies into actions that directly affected the recipients. Local caseworkers, welfare administrators, and supervisors made decisions about how a particular new rule would apply to specific recipient families. Local offices, under guidelines set by the state, were also responsible for much of the data collection related to OBRA. Given the administrative pressures aimed at implementing the policies, data collection was often accorded the lowest priority.

Because of the multiple actors at each level of government, along with the effects of legal services and other advocacy organizations, im-

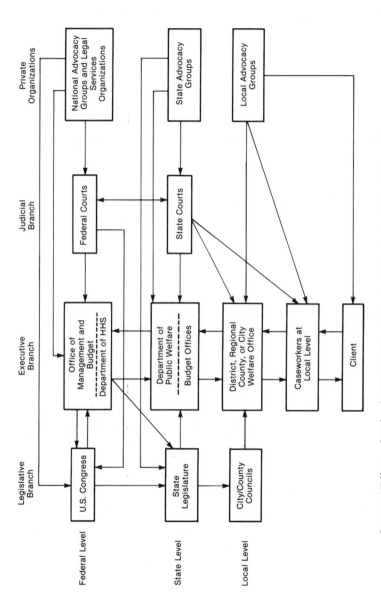

Source: "Effects of Federal AFDC Policy Changes: A Study of a Federal–State Partnership." The Center for the Study of Social Policy, Washington, D.C., 1983.

Figure 5–1. Elements of the Intergovernmental System

plementation of the federal legislation varied widely among states and localities. While this process of reshaping policies at each level of government is characteristic of all matching grant-in-aid entitlement programs, it was particularly acute in the case of the AFDC provisions under OBRA because of the discretion state and local agencies have historically retained in administering the program.

How the AFDC policies were implemented in states can be appreciated only through an understanding of basic intergovernmental relationships in the nation's entitlement programs. In joint federal-state programs, any attempt by the federal government to impose greater control over state-administered programs can tip the balance of control only slightly, and not always in the direction intended. Few policymakers understand the intricate relationships in federal-state programs, and any policy that assumes a straight-line effect between federal directive and local action is likely to achieve far less than anticipated. Thus, the story of how the new federal AFDC rules were implemented illustrates a broader phenomenon. It touches upon a fundamental issue in our federalist system: the role of federal and state governments in ensuring the general welfare of the citizenry.

State Actions Taken to Counteract Federal Policies

When the federal regulations were issued, several state governments took actions to negate or limit the intended effects of the new federal law. Although the federal changes were designed to affect recipients in all states, several states were able to minimize their impact through deliberate state legislative and regulatory strategies. The states sought either to protect recipients or to preserve the nature of the state's AFDC benefit structure. The primary method for doing this was adjustment of states' need standards in relation to their payment standards.

States can modify their need standards and benefit payment levels at any time. Following enactment of the OBRA provision mandating a ceiling on AFDC eligibility at 150 percent of a state's need standard, several states realized that this provision could be offset by raising the need standard. Thus, while an increase in the state need standard would not necessarily alter the level of payments recipients receive, it would allow recipients to earn more income and still be eligible for partial AFDC benefits.

Twenty-seven states took actions to counteract the intended impact of the new rules. Twenty-three states raised their need standards during FY 1982, although not all of them did so deliberately to mitigate the effects of the 150 percent cap. Several states raised their need standard as part of a routine increase. Most of these states raised their need and payment standards proportionately, generally by a fairly small percentage.

At least eight states, however, raised their need standards to avoid terminating thousands of families with earned income—even though this meant that these states would not realize all of the potential cost savings from OBRA. In doing this, the states also sought to prevent the increased costs that could result if recipients who were terminated from AFDC owing to the 150 percent cap returned to the rolls at a higher grant level.

Table 5–1 identifies the major state actions taken. Column (1) of table 5–1 shows seven states that raised only their need standard; of these, Alabama, Iowa, and Massachusetts did so as an explicit reaction to the 150 percent cap. Alabama raised its need standard by 100 percent, the highest increase among these seven states, in order to allow working recipients to remain eligible for AFDC. Column (2) shows those states that raised their need and payment standards equally. Column (3) shows that Florida, Georgia, Maryland, North Carolina, and Pennsylvania raised their payment standard only slightly (less than 10 percent) but increased their need standard substantially.

The most notable example of this strategy is North Carolina, which raised its benefits by only 5 percent but its need standard by 110 percent. In anticipation of OBRA, the North Carolina legislature raised its need standard for a three-person family in October 1981 from $192 to $404 per month. Without such action, all recipients whose gross earnings exceeded $288 per month (150 percent of $192) would have been ineligible for AFDC under the new OBRA rule. With the state legislation, three-person families could have gross incomes up to $606 (150 percent of $404) per month and still be eligible for AFDC. To ensure that this action would not lead to a proportionate increase in benefits to all recipients—a costly action—the state decided to pay only 50 percent of the need standard rather than the 100 percent it had paid before these changes.

Welfare officials in North Carolina estimate that the annual cost of keeping recipients on the rolls who otherwise would have been terminated was approximately $615,000. The state legislature was willing to forgo this amount of potential savings in order to avoid penalizing the working poor in the state.

Table 5–1 also shows those states that changed their payment standards between October 1981 and September 1982. This action not only altered the level of benefits to earners and nonearners alike, but it changed the number of families eligible for benefits. In addition to the sixteen states that raised benefits and their need standard, four states raised only

Table 5–1
State Actions during FY 1982 Which Mitigate Intent of Federal Policies

States	(1) Raised Need Standard Only	(2) Raised Need Standard and Payment Equally	(3) Raised Need Standard More than Payments		(4) Raised Payment Standard Only	(5) Changed Benefit Calculations
			Raised Need Standard	Raise in Payment Standard		
Alabama	100%					
Alaska		7.5%				
Colorado			24%	2.2%		
Connecticut		3%				
District of Columbia[a]		4.1%				
Florida			108%	7.2%		
Georgia			90%	6.0%		
Illinois[b]	61%					
Iowa	15%					
Kansas		3.1%				
Louisiana	9.8%					
Maine		8%				
Maryland			38%	9.3%		X
Massachusetts	5%					
Mississippi	30%					
Missouri					5.2%	
Montana			31%	8.5%		
Nevada					12.4%	
North Carolina			110%	5%		
North Dakota		6.9%				
Ohio	13.5%					
Pennsylvania			71%	5.3%		

South Carolina				
Tennessee				2.8%
Utah				4.4%
Washington[c]	76.5%	9%	4%	X
Wyoming	14.3%			

Source: "Effects of Federal AFDC Policy Changes: A Study of a Federal–State Partnership." The Center for the Study of Social Policy, Washington, D.C., 1983.

[a]D.C. actually revised its payment standard by 4.9 percent but is included in the group that raised their need standards and payment standards by the same amount because the difference is so small.

[b]Illinois created a need standard for the first time in FY 1982. Its 61 percent increase therefore represents the increase over its former payment standard plus an increase in the new need standard.

[c]Washington is somewhat of an alteration for the states that raised their need standard and payment standard proportionally because it was forced by the courts to make a substantial increase in both.

their payment standard. These are shown in Column (4) of the table. In addition, Michigan reduced its maximum benefit by 6 percent soon after implementation of OBRA, and Colorado reduced the percentage of need it paid by 18 percent for seven months before increasing its need standard so that benefits were 2.2 percent higher than they had been before the decrease.

The last column in table 5–1 shows that two states, Maine and Utah, changed their benefit calculation formulas in order to raise benefits to working families who otherwise would have had their benefits reduced owing to termination of the $30 plus one-third disregard under OBRA. These two states changed the methods of calculating benefits in such a way as to increase both the number of eligible recipients with earnings and the amount of the grant paid to the working poor family.[1] Both states changed their policies to provide higher benefits and expanded eligibility to those recipients whose net countable income fell between the payment standard and the need standard. The effect of these actions has been to counteract the new federal policy that eliminated the $30 plus one-third disregard by increasing payments to working recipients.

An illustration of Utah's policy change is useful. Previously, that state's AFDC payment standard amounted to 65.3 percent of its need standard. Grants were calculated by subtracting countable income—that amount of income that is counted dollar for dollar against the AFDC grant—from the payment standard, which was (in 1981) $382 for a family of three. So, for example, a family with $300 in countable income would receive a grant of $82 ($382 minus $300). Effective January 1983, the method of calculating benefits was changed so that countable income is now subtracted from the need standard, which is $584 for a three-person family, and the grant becomes 65.3 percent of the remainder. A family with $300 in countable income thus becomes eligible for a grant of $185 ($584 minus $300, multiplied by .653), as opposed to $82 under the old benefit calculation method. The maximum grant under this new method continues to be $382; however, low-income working families are given a greater financial incentive to work than they were given under the old policy.

These examples illustrate actions taken to reduce the harm anticipated by states as a result of the AFDC provisions affecting wage earners. The actions were also aimed at preventing the possibility of a more costly return of terminated cases (because of reduced work incentives in OBRA) at a later date. In other words, their purpose was to keep working recipients on the rolls so that they would not quit their jobs and reapply for aid at a higher grant level. Because of these actions, the 150 percent cap and the elimination of the $30 plus one-third disregard were not implemented to the extent intended by the federal government.

Administrative Confusion and Delays

Insufficient attention was paid to the administrative complexity of implementing the OBRA provisions when they were enacted. In many states the new administrative apparatus required at the state and local levels was substantial. In fact, in response to a plea from state welfare officials after OBRA was passed, the Department of Health and Human Services agreed not to assess any fiscal penalties on states whose error rates exceeded the allowable maximum—4 percent—attributable to errors related specifically to the federal policy changes. States had to implement not only the new rules affecting working mothers (as outlined in chapter 3) but twenty-two other new rules affecting nonworking clients as well.

Implementation delays are one manifestation of this administrative complexity. Table 5–2 shows the implementation schedules in ten states. As indicated, delays appeared to be the rule rather than the exception. Several reasons account for these delays. First, some states required state

Table 5–2
Implementation Schedules

State	Implementation Schedule
California	Implemented six OBRA provisions December 1981 and remaining provisions May 1982. Already had retrospective budgeting and a form of the stepparent provision. Court order delayed implementation in order to give recipients adequate notice of the changes.
Colorado	Implemented one OBRA provision in October 1981; five provisions in December 1981; two in January 1982. Has received a waiver for monthly reporting.
Georgia	Implemented all provisions October 1981.
Illinois	Implemented all provisions October 1981.
Michigan	Implemented five OBRA provisions October 1981; two in November 1981; one in February 1982. Had implemented stepparent liability policy effective March 1981 but cases were reinstated beginning August 1981 owing to a court order.
Minnesota	Implemented February 1982. Had already passed stepparent liability July 1981.
New York	Implemented in January 1982.
Oklahoma	Implemented all provisions October 1981 except monthly reporting and retrospective budgeting in January 1982.
Pennsylvania	Implemented all provisions November 1981 except stepparent liability September 1982 and monthly reporting April 1983.
Wisconsin	Implemented major components January 1, 1982, after passing necessary state legislation December 1981. Other provisions were implemented February to March. Monthly reporting began October 1982.

Source: "Effects of Federal AFDC Policy Changes: A Study of a Federal–State Partnership." The Center for the Study of Social Policy, Washington, D.C., 1983.

legislation before being able to implement any of the new provisions. For example, Minnesota did not begin implementation until February 1982, after its legislature had revised a state law requiring that actual work expenses be disregarded. Even those states that were able to implement some of the OBRA provisions immediately did not put all of them into effect at once if state legislation was needed. In the case of Pennsylvania, special legislation was required before a provision could be implemented to count stepparents' income, and thus that provision was not implemented until September 1982. A new requirement mandating monthly reporting did not become effective until April 1983 in Pennsylvania.

Other states held up implementing some or all of the provisions because of litigation brought by legal service organizations or client advocacy groups. For example, a California state court issued a preliminary injunction that temporarily blocked implementation of OBRA until the Department of Social Services fulfilled the state Administrative Procedures Act (APA) by giving public notice of the changes.[2] However, California was able to avoid the requirements of its own APA when the state legislature enacted the proposed regulations on an emergency basis. Courts in Hawaii, Louisiana, and New Mexico also delayed implementation of OBRA.[3]

In addition to implementation delays, several specific provisions proved particularly troublesome for administrators. The one requiring stepparents to be financially responsible for their stepchildren caused confusion in several states. Prior to OBRA, most states were prohibited from considering the income of stepparents in determining AFDC eligibility and grant amounts. The OBRA stepparent rule reversed this by mandating that the income of a stepparent (minus certain deductions) must be considered available to the family. A stepparent is defined in the regulations as a person who is ceremonially married to the child's parent under state law. But it was not made clear whether common-law marriages in states that recognize such marriages would constitute a stepparent case. A court case is pending on this issue in Kansas. The state of New York sent caseworkers eight pages of detailed instructions to guide implementation of this one provision.

The provision most often cited as burdensome is the one that mandates monthly reporting. Under OBRA, all recipients were required to report their income each month, whereas states were free to require reports on a quarterly basis prior to 1981. State welfare officials had renounced previous federal proposals mandating monthly reporting because of the substantial paperwork required and the administrative costs associated with the proposals. For the first time in many states, recipients had to complete highly complex and confusing forms. Furthermore, because many recipients are terminated when they fail to complete a monthly form, a large number of them end up being reinstated a month or two later. This simply adds to the administrative burden at the local level. For instance, Oklahoma estimated that the 5,386 cases closed over seven months in 1982 for failure to submit a monthly reporting form, 1,587 of them (or 29 percent) were recertified *within the same month* as their closure; 93 percent returned to the rolls within thirteen months.

A provision reducing allowable resources from $2,000 to $1,000 was also particularly difficult to administer. The limit on resources can be implemented only if caseworkers visit each recipient family's home, since under the new law caseworkers must determine the equity value of all belongings. Because of the inevitable ambiguity in establishing equity values and the time needed to make home visits, few caseworkers carried out this provision fully. Most often the provision was ignored.

Judicial Interpretations

There was also substantial judicial action directly shaping the way in which the federal AFDC policy changes were applied. Dozens of court decisions in numerous states directed state welfare agencies to revise their methods of implementing the new rules, and in several cases agencies were forced to make massive retrospective changes. A few of the major ones are described here and are summarized in table 5–3.

The 150 percent cap provision provoked several lawsuits. For example, a federal district court in Pennsylvania issued a decision ordering the states to calculate the 150 percent cap by referring to the state's full need standard rather than another standard they were using that was on average 71 percent lower. The state was ordered to "restore all AFDC and Medicaid benefits improperly withheld."[4] Similarly, a state court in Florida issued a preliminary injunction prohibiting any terminations based on the 150 percent cap because of the inadequacy of Florida's need standard, which had not been raised since 1970.[5]

The provision standardizing the work-expense disregard at $75 also caused considerable controversy. In this case, different courts have ruled in opposition to each other, so that the rule is being applied differently in various states. A federal district court in New York issued a preliminary injunction ordering the state to apply the disregard *after* subtracting mandatory deductions such as income taxes and Social Security taxes. Thus, the recipient receives a $75 work-expense deduction in addition to actual mandatory deductions on the premise that mandatory deductions cannot be considered income.[6] Because of this ruling, the New York Department of Social Services was forced to restore eligibility to clients

Table 5–3
Judicial Interpretations Affecting the Implementation of OBRA

	Court Orders on 150% Cap	Court Orders on $75 Work Disregard	Court Orders on Stepparents	Court Orders on Lump Sums	Court Orders on Medicaid Terminations
Arizona				Does not apply to lump sums received by stepparents or in life-threatening circumstances.	
California		$75 disregard to be applied to net earnings rather than gross.			Must continue coverage of Medicaid four months after AFDC terminations.
Florida	Prohibited terminations because of inadequate need standard that had not been revised since 1970.				
Indiana	Must use full standard of need rather than payment standard, which was 90 percent of need.				Does not have to continue Medicaid coverage four months after termination of AFDC.
Kansas			Court order pending on application to common-law marriages.		
Maine		$75 disregard to be applied to gross earnings rather than net.			

State					
Michigan					
New York		$75 disregard to be applied to net earnings rather than gross.	Disallows stepparent liability in August 1981 because conflicts with federal law.	Must be available and only applies to earners.	Requires separate eligibility determinations for medically needy before AFDC and General Assistance terminations.
Pennsylvania	Must use Woodbury full need standard rather than payment standard.	$75 disregard to be applied to gross income rather than net.			
Rhode Island				Treats proceeds from sale of a resource as resource rather than lump sum.	

Source: "Effects of Federal AFDC Policy Changes: A Study of a Federal–State Partnership." The Center for the Study of Social Policy, Washington, D.C., 1983.

terminated between January and March 1982 on account of the $75 work-expense deduction. A federal district court in California agreed,[7] but a court in Maine ruled that the $75 disregard included all mandatory deductions and therefore could not be applied in addition to them.[8] In 1984, Congress finally clarified its intent, defining income as gross income and requiring the application of the work-expense deduction to income before taxes are subtracted. This reversed the New York and California court rulings.

Other court decisions have also resulted in increased benefits to recipients. OBRA mandated termination of recipients who had any "lump sum" income that exceeded the state need standard. For the first time, OBRA counted as income any payments received by recipients such as an inheritance or a one-time disability payment. The AFDC grant was reduced over a period of time according to the amount of the payment. Formerly, such one-time payments, if spent, did not reduce the grant. A federal court in Michigan, however, issued a preliminary injunction favoring a recipient's claim that the income must be "actually available" to the family.[9] In an Arizona case, the state agreed to add a provision to its rules manual allowing families to receive AFDC if a life-threatening circumstance occurs during the lump-sum disqualification period.[10] Similarly, a federal district court in Rhode Island issued a consent order in which the state welfare agency agreed to treat the proceeds from the sale of a resource as a resource rather than as income.[11] In each of these instances, benefits were reinstated to terminated recipients following the court order.

Finally, several court decisions affected the termination of Medicaid benefits to families removed from the AFDC rolls. Because Medicaid is automatically tied to AFDC eligibility, families who became ineligible for AFDC were often dropped immediately from Medicaid as well. A California court issued a preliminary injunction ordering the state to continue Medicaid coverage for four months for all AFDC recipients terminated because of changes in the counting of earned income. This ruling was based on the plaintiffs' claim that federal law mandates continued Medicaid coverage for four months after AFDC terminations owing to increased income from employment.[12] However, a court in Indiana rejected the same notion.[13]

These court decisions attest to the variability with which the new federal rules were carried out in each state. Individually and cumulatively, these and other court cases affected the state welfare caseloads at any given point in time. As a result, the way in which recipients were affected by the new policies was not consistent across states.

In summary, many factors at each level of government shaped the way in which the new AFDC policies were implemented and ultimately affected clients. State actions to change need standards, payment standards, and calculation formulas were taken in twenty-seven states and the District of Columbia, mitigating the intended effects of OBRA. Administrative complexity at the state and local levels delayed implementation in several states. Courts ordered substantial reinstatement of benefits and issued rulings that were, in some cases, contradictory to court rulings in other states. Because there was no direct path leading from the federal legislation to the client, the new rules were implemented in varying ways across states. To make matters worse, implementation at the local level varied even more. The next chapter shows how the changes were implemented in one county in one state.

Notes

1. Maine passed legislation to accomplish this objective in 1982, and Utah implemented this change through administrative action in January 1983.
2. *Clutchette* v. *Brown,* California Superior court, City of Los Angeles, 1981. The Center of Social Welfare Policy and Law is the best source of information on welfare litigation. The cases cited in this chapter are summarized in three memos issued by the center, dated February 3, May 7, and December 9, 1982.
3. *Costa* v. *Sunn,* Hawaii Superior Court, 16 March 1982.
4. *Coleman* v. *O'Bannon,* Federal District Court, E.D., Pennsylavania, 1981.
5. *Goldbold* v. *Pingree,* Florida Circuit Court, 2d Circuit, 1982.
6. *R.A.M.* v. *Blum,* Federal District Court, S.D., New York, 1982.
7. *Turner* v. *Woods,* Federal District Court, N.D., California, 1982.
8. *Dickenson* v. *Petit,* Federal District court, D., Maine, 1982.
9. *Vermeulen* v. *Kheder and Schweiker,* Federal District Court, W.D., Michigan, 1982.
10. *Hermandex* v. *Jamieson,* Federal District Court, D., Arizona, 1982.
11. *Rochford* v. *Affleck,* Federal District Court, D., Rhode Island, 1982.
12. *Edwards* v. *Myers,* Superior Court, County of Los Angeles, 1982.
13. *Jones* v. *Blinziger,* Federal District Court, N.D., Indiana.

6
Implementation at the Local Level

Once the new policies filtered down from the federal government through the states, it was up to the local welfare offices to put the policies into operation. It was at this level that the new rules were translated into dollar losses or gains for individual families.

AFDC has always been difficult to administer because of the large number of eligibility and benefit rules. Determining how much money a family will receive requires a lengthy review of its financial circumstances. In addition, caseworkers must continuously monitor the family's income so that the grant can be adjusted accordingly. Given the number of changes that routinely occur in one's personal life—a move, the birth of a child, a change in a job, a child turning eighteen and leaving home, and so forth—caseworkers are constantly recalculating each family's grant.

Moreover, AFDC spans three layers of government—federal, state, and local. In addition, AFDC has provided for working as well as non-working families who meet its eligibility requirements. In essence, AFDC has functioned both as a "safety net" for those without any income and as a helping hand upward for those on their way out of poverty. In short, the administrative burdens on caseworkers and clients have always been enormous, and the time required for routine grant changes considerable.

The 1981 legislative changes served to make an already complex program even more intricate for caseworkers and clients alike. The implementation of OBRA at the local level illustrates the fact that policy-makers compounded the complexity of AFDC through their reforms. The Reagan administration argued that the 1981 welfare changes would make the system more "target efficient." In doing this, however, the changes neither simplified procedures nor reduced the burden of paperwork. In fact, as shown on the following pages, the changes greatly complicated an already complex set of procedures at the local level.

To document the local administrative difficulties both before and after OBRA, we examined a typical AFDC family in Georgia. Our analysis of this family's ride through the welfare system between 1980 and 1983 looks closely at the actual program procedures from the prospective of the worker-client interaction. It is not enough to scrutinize federal rules and regulations; in order to reveal their true effects, it is necessary to see how the rules are actually carried out. We do so in the following pages through Anna Burns and her family.

The story of Anna Burns and her caseworker is taken from the AFDC and food stamp records of a real family. Only the name is changed. Ms. Burns's family is typical of other families on welfare, with two exceptions: (1) Ms. Burns is one of the lucky few to find a job, and (2) she lives in a small town instead of in an urban area, where most AFDC families live. The family's story offers a glimpse into the detailed operations of AFDC both before and after OBRA.

For years, scholars and policy analysts have talked about how we can deliver welfare services and dispense benefits more efficiently and effectively. Yet this discussion is meaningless unless we first understand the particulars that Anna Burns's story conveys. Only through an understanding of the procedures that caseworkers and clients currently must go through on a monthly basis can we hope to make sense of the so-called policy reforms that form the core of this book.

Anna Burns

September 1980: Anna Burns is a divorced twenty-eight-year-old mother of three living in a small town in Georgia. Ms. Burns's eldest daughter is entering the sixth grade, and the twins are entering fifth grade. Ms. Burns supports her family through a combination of wages, occasional support from her ex-husband, and public assistance.

At this time, Ms. Burns is unemployed but is actively seeking a job. She and her three children receive $193 monthly in AFDC, $201 in food stamps, and health insurance through the Medicaid program. She must make an appointment with her caseworker at the county welfare office every six months, unless she begins working, in which case she must notify her caseworker within ten days.

Monthly family income from AFDC and food stamps: $394.00.

November 1980: Ms. Burns is offered a job as a nurse's assistant in a nursing home not far from where she lives. She accepts the position, begins working, and, as required, reports this change to her caseworker. The caseworker requests documentation of her earnings, taxes, travel, and child-care costs, and of the cost of the uniform she must wear at work. Ms. Burns files a written statement indicating how many miles she drives to and from work and another written statement from the neighbor who looks after her children declaring how much the neighbor receives for caring for the three girls. Ms. Burns sends these documents to her caseworker for a redetermination of her eligibility for AFDC and food stamps.

In addition to the above information required by the AFDC program, the food stamp program requires documentation of rent, telephone, and utility expenses. Altogether, Ms. Burns must provide, and her caseworker must review, eight documents this month.

The caseworker receives Ms. Burns's information and calculates that her client's gross monthly earnings total $546. The caseworker must then make two determinations: one, whether Ms. Burns is eligible for a grant, given her earnings, and two, if so, how much her monthly grant will be. Once her client meets the family composition and assets test, the caseworker compares Anna Burns's income to the state need standard. To determine the payment amount, the caseworker compares Ms. Burns's income with the payment standard. As shown in chapter 2, the need standard determines eligibility; the payment standard determines benefit amount and in many states is below the need standard. In Georgia, the payment standard is half of the need standard. In other words, while the state said a family of four required $432 monthly to cover minimum needs in 1984, it would provide such a family with no income only $216 in AFDC. A family with some income receives the difference between the payment standard and its countable income. Therefore, if the family's countable income is greater than the payment standard, it cannot receive AFDC.

In determining eligibility for Anna Burns's family, the caseworker uses the following formula:

Work expenses of $50 and child-chare expenses of $87 (total: $137) are subtracted from Ms. Burns's gross wages: $546 − $137 = $409.

The $409 is then compared to the need standard for a family of four, which was $227 in November 1980. Because the $409 exceeds the need standard, Ms. Burns is *not* eligible for AFDC.

Since Ms. Burns's family is not eligible for a grant, the caseworker of course does not have to proceed to the second step and calculate how much her grant would be.

The caseworker sends Ms. Burns a notice that effective December 1, 1980, she will no longer receive AFDC, on account of her new earnings. Her eligibility for Medicaid, however, will continue for four months, as mandated by federal law.

Because Ms. Burns is now working, her caseworker must reassess her food stamp case as well. Many counties have separate AFDC and food stamp case units, assigning two caseworkers to a single family. Ms.

Burns, however, lives in a small county that has no separate program staffs, and the same caseworker monitors Ms. Burns's AFDC case and her food stamp case.

Applying the food stamp program formula to Ms. Burns's new income, the caseworker calculates that her client is eligible for $127 in food stamps, compared to $201 during the previous month. The following calculations apply:

Earned income of $546, less a 20 percent (or $109) work disregard;

Less a standard earnings deduction of $75;

Less child-care costs of $87; and

Less a shelter deduction of $3 ($3 is the maximum Ms. Burns is entitled to, regardless of her actual shelter expenses, owing to a $90 ceiling on combined dependent care and shelter deductions).

The result is then multiplied by .3 and subtracted from the Thrifty Food Plan ($209 for a four-person family in 1980).

$$\$209 - [(\$546 - \$109 - \$75 - \$87 - \$3).3] = \$127$$

Thus, Ms. Burns will now receive $127 in food stamps. The caseworker must send Ms. Burns a second notice indicating this change in her food stamp allotment.

Monthly family income of gross wages and food stamps: $673.00.

February 1981: Ms. Burns must reduce her hours at work. She immediately contacts her caseworker to report the change in her earnings and expenses; she mails in her new pay stubs. The caseworker calculates her earnings to be $350 per month, her work expenses to be $88, and her child-care expenses to be $38. She then proceeds to determine whether Ms. Burns is now eligible for AFDC, and, if so, how much her payment will be.

The caseworker finds that Ms. Burns is eligible for aid because her gross income minus work and child-care expenses ($350 − $88 − $38 = $224) is less than the need standard of $227. In order to determine the amount of her payment, the caseworker applies a second formula:

First, she subtracts $30 from the total earnings ($350 − $30 = $320).

Second, the remaining income is reduced by one-third, leaving $213. The effect of this $30 and one-third earnings disregard, mandated by federal law, is to reduce the amount of earned income that the welfare agency considers when calculating the family's AFDC grant. The intent is to provide welfare recipients with an incentive to work.

Third, the caseworker subtracts $88 to account for income taxes, uniforms, travel expenses, meal expenses, and other customary work expenses. (If Ms. Burns could not document these expenses, she would be given a standard deduction of $50.)

The caseworker next subtracts Ms. Burns's child-care expenses, which total $38 monthly.

$$(\$350 - \$30) - [1/3 \ (\$320 - \$30)] - \$88 - \$38 = \$87$$

The remaining income, $87, is considered to be Ms. Burns's countable income and is subtracted from the payment standard—$193 for a family of four—to reach the AFDC grant amount ($193 − $87 = $106).

Because of the significant decrease in her earnings, Ms. Burns is again eligible for AFDC, effective the following month. The caseworker sends a notice indicating that Ms. Burns will begin receiving an AFDC grant of $106 in March.

The caseworker must also redetermine Ms. Burns's eligibility for food stamps because of the change in her earnings, expenses, and AFDC status. Accounting for these changes, the caseworker determines that Ms. Burns's food stamp allotment should increase to $171 in March.

Monthly family income of gross wages, AFDC and food stamps: $627.

June 1981: The state of Georgia increases its AFDC payment standard. Consequently, all AFDC cases must be reviewed and all grants increased according to the new schedule. The caseworker calculates that Ms. Burns's grant should increase from $126 to $140, effective in July. This in turn requires an adjustment of Ms. Burns's food stamp allotment. Accounting for the increase in her AFDC grant, Ms. Burns's food stamp allotment decreases from $171 to $160.

Monthly family income: $650.

September 1981: In July, the U.S. Congress passes the Omnibus Budget Reconciliation Act, mandating a number of significant AFDC and food stamp policy changes. Because the changes are both numerous and complex, caseworkers are summoned in each county for special training sessions. These federal policy changes require that the caseworkers review each case assigned to them, make the necessary changes, and notify their clients of these changes.

Ms. Burns's caseworker reviews each of the 85 AFDC and 200 food stamp cases assigned to her and adjusts their grants on the basis of the new policies. During this time, Ms. Burns receives a pay increase and is able to increase her hours at the nursing home. She reports these changes to her caseworker by sending in her most recent pay stubs. The caseworker calculates that Ms. Burns's monthly earnings have increased from $350 to $438. Many of the next steps in the method of calculating Ms. Burns's grant have changed as a result of OBRA.

> First, the caseworker must now determine whether a family's total income, before deductions, is within a new set of limits created by federal law.

This new federal rule, called the "150 percent cap," requires that in order to be eligible, a family's gross income (before taxes, child-care, and any other deductions are taken) must be no greater than 150 percent of the state's need standard. If a family's total income is greater than 150 percent of the state's need standard, the family is automatically ineligible for AFDC (and in many states, Medicaid), regardless of the family's work or living expenses.

Ms. Burns's income is within the new limits, so she remains eligible. The limit in Georgia for a family of four after the state raised its eligibility ceiling is $648 and Ms. Burns's total income is only $438. So the calculations proceed:

> Next the caseworker subtracts from Ms. Burns's earnings the new standard work expense deduction of $75, and her child-care expenses of $36.

> Finally, the caseworker applies the $30 and one-third earnings deduction to the remaining income. Prior to OBRA this deduction had been applied to the total earnings; now it is applied to earnings less work expenses. The result is a smaller grant for all working AFDC recipients. The caseworker calculates Ms. Burns's countable income as $198.

$$\$438 - \$75 - \$36 - \$30 - [\ 1/3\ (\$438 - \$75 - \$36 - \$30] = \$198$$

This countable income is compared to the state payment standard of $216, which was increased from $193 in July 1981. Ms. Burns qualifies for an $18 payment ($216 − $198 = $18). Thus Ms. Burns's grant is reduced from $140 to $18, effective October, and the caseworker sends out a notice indicating the reason for the change and the new grant amount. As a result of the change in Ms. Burns's AFDC grant and her increased wages, her caseworker must also recalculate her food stamp benefits. Because of the reduced AFDC grant, Ms. Burns's food stamp allotment increases from $160 to $183, effective October 1. Ms. Burns receives a second notice from her caseworker showing the new food stamp allotment.

Monthly family income from wages, AFDC, and food stamps: $639.

November 1981: Caseworkers are instructed that OBRA has mandated a change in the earned income deduction in the food stamp program: it is to be reduced from 20 percent of earned income to 18 percent. The caseworker must recalculate the food stamp budget for each case in which the household has earned income. The effect on Ms. Burns's food stamp allotment is small, as in most cases: a reduction from $183 to $180 in coupons.

Monthly family income: $636.

January 1982: OBRA mandates that the $30 and one-third earnings disregard be limited to four months in any twelve-month period. Consequently, Ms. Burns's caseworker determines that as of February, she will no longer be entitled to this earnings disregard. Because this new policy took effect in October, Ms. Burns was entitled to the disregard for the four months beginning in October. The caseworker recalculates Ms. Burns's February grant as follows:

$$
\begin{array}{rl}
\$\ 438 & \text{earnings} \\
-75 & \text{standard deduction} \\
\hline
\$\ 363 & \\
-36 & \text{child-care expenses} \\
\hline
\$\ 327 &
\end{array}
$$

Expiration of the $30 and one-third disregard increases Ms. Burns's countable income from $198 to $327, well above the payment standard of $216, thereby making her ineligible for AFDC and Medicaid.

The caseworker sends Ms. Burns a letter indicating that her AFDC grant will terminate effective February 1, 1982, because of the new federal policy limiting the $30 and one-third earnings disregard to four months. Ms. Burns will also lose her Medicaid coverage as a direct result of becoming ineligible for AFDC.

Because Ms. Burns's AFDC case must be closed, her food stamp case must be reevaluated and the AFDC benefits removed from the food stamp budget. In January 1982, as the caseworker is calculating a new food stamp allotment, Ms. Burns sends her caseworker her most recent series of pay stubs, indicating a small increase in her wages. The caseworker determines that Ms. Burns's earnings have increased from $438 to $454. This increase in earnings, despite the loss of AFDC benefits, results in a decrease in food stamp benefits from $180 to $167.

Monthly family income of earnings plus food stamps: $621.

February 1982: Because Ms. Burns fails to document her rent, utilities, and child-care expenses, the caseworker cannot give Ms. Burns credit for having any such expenses in calculating the family's food stamp allotment. The end result is a reduced food stamp allotment. As the caseworker is calculating the reduction, Ms. Burns once again notifies her that her earnings have increased to $511. As a result of Ms. Burns's increased earnings and her failure to document her household expenses, the family's food stamp allotment decreases from $167 to $133 in March.

Monthly family income: $644.

June 1982: Ms. Burns's eldest daughter gives birth. Because the new mother is under sixteen years of age, Ms. Burns applies for an AFDC grant on behalf of her granddaughter. The Burns family receives no support from the father of the new baby, and the baby's mother, who has just completed the seventh grade, is unable to support the child. Thus, the child is eligible for an AFDC grant amounting to $107, payable to Ms. Burns. Only the child is eligible for AFDC and Medicaid. Ms. Burns's earnings are not considered in calculating her grandchild's grant, and she is not considered financially responsible for this child under the AFDC program.

During this same month, Ms. Burns's earnings decrease from $511 to $470. The caseworker recalculates Ms. Burns's food stamp allotment on the basis of her new level of earnings and the additional household member; however, the AFDC grant is not calculated into the budget until the following month. The result is an increase in the family's food stamp allotment from $133 to $188 in July. However, in August, the food stamp allotment decreases to $155, accounting for the additional AFDC income of $107. Each change requires written notification from the caseworker to Ms. Burns.

Monthly family income: $732 for a family of five.

September 1982: Federal law mandates an increase in the food stamp allotment ceilings and the telephone and utilities deductions. Ms. Burns's caseworker must review each of the 200 food stamp cases assigned to her and recalculate their food stamp allotments using the new dollar figures mandated by the federal government. Ms. Burns's allotment increases from $155 to $177, effective October.

Monthly family income: $754.

October 1982: Georgia implements a final OBRA policy change in the AFDC program. Were Ms. Burns still eligible for an AFDC grant for herself and her daughters, she would now be required to report her wages and income each and every month. Failure to comply with this new requirement would result in the termination of benefits.

The monthly reporting requirement consumes an inordinate amount of time for caseworkers. The client must fill out and mail in a form reporting all earnings. The form must be postmarked between the first and the fifth days of the month. If it is mailed before the first day of the month, it cannot be accepted and the caseworker must mail it back to the client and have her resubmit it. If it is not received by the sixth day of the month, the caseworker must mail the client a reminder to send it in. If it is not received by the fifteenth of the month, benefits are terminated. In the relatively small office where Anna Burns's case is staffed, one social worker spends two weeks every month doing nothing but making sure all the monthly reports are received properly. Each caseworker must then review the forms on his or her caseload and make any necessary adjustments.

December 1982: Ms. Burns's pay stubs indicate yet another small change in her level of earnings, requiring her caseworker to recalculate her family's food stamp allotment and send Ms. Burns the appropriate notification. The earnings change is an increase of $17 monthly, from $470 to $487. The corresponding change in the family's food stamp allotment is a $4 decrease, from $177 to $173 in January 1983.

Monthly family income: $767.

March 1983: Ms. Burns sends her caseworker copies of her rent and utility bills, which are considerably higher than in previous months, together with pay stubs indicating a small decrease in earnings. The family now lives on Ms. Burns's before-tax earnings of $474, her granddaughter's AFDC grant of $107, food stamps amounting to $192, and a very occasional $15 child-support payment from Ms. Burns's ex-husband.

Monthly family gross income: $773.

Policy Implications

The history of the Burns family's participation in the AFDC and food stamp programs documents the administrative complexity of these programs. In thirty-two months, Anna Burns's AFDC grant had to be re-calculated fourteen times, her food stamp grant recalculated fourteen times (see figure 6–1), and her Medicaid eligibility changed four times. Yet the family's total income changed very little. In attempting to make the level of benefits reflect the family's ever-changing circumstances, the programs require extensive and continuous documentation of income, expenses, and family composition by the recipient. This in turn requires close and constant monitoring by the caseworker, together with the considerable amount of paperwork required to adjust grants month by month as the family's circumstances change.

Each application for AFDC or change in earnings requires that a great deal of time, energy, and money be expended. The initial AFDC application form consists of nearly ten pages of detailed questions. Ms. Burns must go to the welfare office at the time of application, sixty days later for a review, and every six months thereafter as long as she remains on welfare. To make those visits, she must take time off from work, thereby reducing her earnings and risking the displeasure of her superiors. In between these periods she may report her earnings and expenses by mail.

From the caseworker's point of view, every change in earnings re-

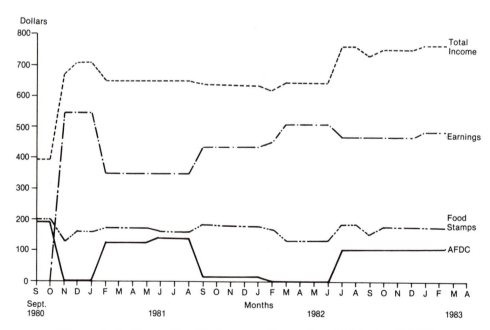

Figure 6–1. Burns Family Income: September 1980–April 1983

quires forty-five minutes' to an hour's work to fill out the proper form. This is submitted to a computer operator, who spends fifteen to twenty minutes entering the information. This is then sent to the state office and returned two days later in printed form. The caseworker must then spend another fifteen to twenty minutes double-checking the form for mistakes. In the example of Ms. Burns, her caseworker had another eighty-four AFDC clients requiring many of the same calculations.

Anna Burns's family is only one family in one county in one state. In 1981–82 there were 3.8 million other families receiving AFDC throughout the country, 500,000 of whom were working families like Anna Burns's whose grants were continually adjusted. The difficulties faced by Anna Burns and her caseworker are typical of many more families who found that their benefits constantly fluctuated in response to unexplained and often little understood policy changes.

It is readily apparent that the 1981 changes only further complicated an already complex system. Instead of helping to simplify administration, the changes only meant more benefit changes and more paperwork both for caseworkers and clients.

On top of this, the federal government imposed stiff penalties on states whose error rates exceeded a specified level. Given the number of calculations that are typically performed, it is amazing that error rates are not higher than they are. But it is a cruelly ironic twist for the federal government to simultaneously complicate the eligibility and benefit calculation process and then impose sanctions on states that make mistakes in calculating benefits.

The story of Anna Burns illustrates the wide gulf that exists between ideological debates on welfare reform and their effect on individual clients. Conceptually it is difficult to oppose objectives of targeting, efficiency, and accountability. The difficulty arises in translating these objectives into sensible and sensitive actions without incurring unintended negative consequences. It is this leap from concept to practice that is rarely given adequate forethought and that was ignored when the AFDC changes were legislated in 1981.

Anna Burns's story also suggests that policymakers need to balance the costs and benefits of increased targeting. Government may be spending too much time and money keeping benefits in step with marginal changes in recipients' financial circumstances: even the normal level of complexity in the welfare system is staggering. In Georgia, it now costs $31 in administrative expenses to process and deliver an average monthly AFDC check of $176.00.[2] And this does not include the administrative costs of recalculating and delivering food stamps.

We are not suggesting that limited resources be squandered on those who do not need assistance. However, at some point, the costs of recalculating benefits outweigh the utility of doing so. There is a trade-off between maximum targeting of benefits and creating a program that is so unmanageable that it is ineffective organizationally as well as insensitive to individual circumstances. The example of Anna Burns suggests that this is a far more serious problem than most reformers have realized.

Given the difficulties demonstrated by this case study, it is no wonder past attempts at welfare reform have failed. When we see how terribly complex it is to deliver AFDC and food stamps to Anna Burns and know that this is replayed in thousands of counties across fifty states, we can readily understand the difficulty policymakers face when they set out to reform the welfare system. If future policy changes are to make the system more effective and efficient, they must be grounded in a detailed understanding of how the system works for both clients and caseworkers. The question that must be addressed is, how can large-scale organizatons like federal, state, and county welfare offices make changes in an intergovernmental program like AFDC?

The answer to this question is not simple. But an understanding of Anna Burns's situation and others like hers must be incorporated into the policy-making process as baseline knowledge. Otherwise, future incremental or structural changes may—like OBRA—only make the welfare system more complex rather than more responsive. Only with this baseline knowledge can we expect to strike a proper balance between the demands placed on a large bureaucracy for administrative efficiency and the most personal of goals: meeting the basic income-support needs of low-income families.

Notes

1. This chapter is reprinted with permission of the American Public Welfare Association from an article printed in *Public Welfare* 43, no. 1 (Winter 1985). Copyright 1985 by the American Public Welfare Association.

2. "Background Material and Data on Programs Within the Jurisdiction of the Committee on Ways and Means," Committee Print, WMCP:98-22, U.S. Government Printing Office, Washington, D.C., February 21, 1984. table 14, 297.

Part III
Effects

7
Research Findings on the Impact of the Policy Changes

S hortly after the policy changes were implemented in October 1981, the administration began to claim that the new rules were successfully achieving their objectives. The new policies, it was asserted, had (1) saved dollars both for the federal government and for states, (2) increased the administrative efficiency of AFDC, simultaneously making the program more easily managed and less subject to fraud and abuse, and (3) returned the AFDC program to its "original intentions" of helping the truly needy. The success of the new law was used as the basis for promoting similar changes in AFDC for FY 1983 and FY 1984.

A closer examination of the implementation of the new policies from 1982 to 1983 reveals a picture that is much different from the one painted by the administration at that time.

To see how OBRA was implemented and what impact it had on caseloads and budgets, we visited ten state welfare offices one year after the new policies took effect. We chose to start at the state level because states had the responsibility of implementing the policy changes and because they established the specifications by which local administrators recorded their actions. We therefore reasoned that states would be the best sources for determining the effects of the new policies on caseloads and budgets. The ten states included in the study were California, Colorado, Georgia, Illinois, Michigan, Minnesota, New York, Oklahoma, Pennsylvania, and Wisconsin.

Originally, our intention was to use state caseload and budget data to answer, in quantitative terms, the following key questions: How many families were terminated from AFDC on account of the federal policy changes, and how many had their benefits reduced? What percentage of terminated families later returned to the AFDC rolls? What has been the budgetary impact of these case actions? But after visiting ten states and examining how OBRA was implemented in each, it became apparent that the available data fell far short of answering these questions. This was due primarily to states' inability to generate data on the policy changes. Moreover, the unique conditions surrounding the implementation of the new federal policies in each state meant that each one's data reflected a different situation. The variations among states were so great that data were not comparable across states, and a national statistical profile of OBRA's effects could not be derived. Thus, it became apparent that the evidence to support the administration's sweeping statements about the merits of the new law simply did not exist. The claims advanced by the administration may have been based on political strategy, ideology, or wishful thinking, but they could not have been based on data because, with few exceptions, the data necessary to substantiate such claims were not available at that time. Furthermore, the fragmentary and incomplete data that were available indicated that the impact of OBRA was much more mixed than was indicated by the administration's claims. On whatever dimension OBRA was judged, conclusions must be tentative, recognizing the ambiguity of the data that were produced by states and acknowledging the complexity of the intergovernmental process that was set in motion by OBRA's enactment.

The ten-state study demonstrated that the data necessary to assess OBRA's impact fully were simply not available from states. The statistics produced by states were incomplete and thus not sufficient to portray the national impact of the legislation. In some cases, even the limited data available were known to be inaccurate. Several factors account for these limitations.

The first problem is that data, limited as they were, varied considerably from state to state. Of the ten states studied, for example, each had collected some data on the budgetary and caseload impact of the new federal policies, but the extent and nature of the data were not uniform across states. Some states merely collected routine data, giving OBRA little special attention because state officials were too pressed with program operations to give priority to documenting the process and outcome of program change. There has always been a certain tension between program administrators who believe that research is nice, but not of central concern to the more important task of operating a program, and researchers who view administrators as shortsighted and caught up in their own narrow operational world. When OBRA came into being, the demands for swift changes in program operations were so great that there was little, if any, time for research or evaluation. A few of the ten states had the capacity to produce special computer runs to provide additional information on the effects of OBRA (for example, Oklahoma and Pennsylvania had considerable raw data), but in most states this opportunity did not exist because the source data had never been collected. When OBRA was implemented, the Department of Health and Human Services mandated uniform reporting requirements for all states, but the information obtained from these has not been sufficient even to judge cost and caseload effects fully.

Moreover, states carried out these mandates differently. For example, all states were required to provide information on the number of terminations due to federal policy changes, but the accuracy of these statistics varied widely. Some states collected actual counts from caseworkers while others merely made estimates based on samples or caseload projections. Similarly, states' estimates of benefit reductions and net budgetary impact were derived in many different ways, making it impossible to aggregate data across states or to compare the effects of OBRA from one state to another.

This scarcity of data was symptomatic of a large, ongoing, and more pervasive difficulty: state public assistance data systems are generally ill-equipped to measure the impact of policy changes. Many state systems are still being designed to enable them to track recipients, benefits, and eligibility information reliably. Attempting to derive evaluative data from the systems usually overloads their capacities. For example, in trying to assess the impact of each of the specific provisions of OBRA, most states found their data systems inadequate. Of the ten states we examined, only Pennsylvania could relate case actions to each of the specific OBRA provisions. This information was not published, however, because the computer system could not be freed from the routine administration of the program long enough to produce an evaluation of OBRA.

In most states, differentiation was made among only a few of the OBRA provisions, or among a few clusters of related provisions. For example, in the months following OBRA's implementation, Oklahoma distinguished only three types of case closings: (1) termination due to "change in policy" (OBRA), (2) termination due to retrospective budgeting, and (3) termination due to reasons unrelated to OBRA. This was fairly typical of most of the ten states examined.

Even in states that did attempt to differentiate more systematically among the OBRA provisions, officials admitted a high degree of error or inconsistency. For example, in Michigan, caseworkers sometimes coded cases that were closed because of the 150 percent cap as "excess income" cases, and other times as a change in policy. In Georgia, a similar inconsistency existed between cases that were coded as closed by virtue of the 150 percent cap on income, on the one hand, and the stepparent provision, on the other.

Data were also lacking because of confounding economic and demographic complexities. Researchers are seldom able to isolate the effects of policies or programs on beneficiaries in light of exogenous forces at play in the environment. In the case of AFDC, much of the research conducted in the past has been confined to examining caseload cycles rather than the relationship between caseload and external economic and societal forces.

An examination of OBRA's effects in each state is complicated by this same problem. The most obvious difficulty is the general economic condition and, specifically, the effect of unemployment rates in each state. It is likely that high unemployment rates increase caseload size and budgets as well as rates of recidivism, although the literature suggests there is generally a delayed reaction between unemployment and caseload growth. Yet it is not known exactly how much the unemployment rate affects the caseload patterns in each state and locality.

For example, a study in New York, although not directly related to AFDC, showed that the increase in the state General Assistance (GA) caseload was highest in those counties with the highest unemployment rates. (General Assistance is a cash assistance program for the poor operated by some states and localities; it generally serves single persons and childless couples who are not eligible for AFDC.) Between March 1981 and March 1982, the four counties in upstate New York with the highest unemployment rates in the state showed a 19.3 percent increase in their GA caseload. The four counties with the lowest unemployment rates in the state showed a GA increase of only 8 percent. This phenomenon is likely to occur in other states as well. If the level of unemployment has a direct bearing on the number of people who apply for and receive General Assistance in New York, it is likely to have the same type of effect on AFDC caseloads. As such, it is an important variable that must be taken into account when analyzing the impact of OBRA on AFDC recipients. To the extent that unemployment is ignored, data on changes in the employment status of former and current AFDC recipients will remain inadequate.

Other exogenous forces that play an important role in AFDC caseload characteristics hampered state efforts to evaluate the impact of OBRA in 1981. These include the following:

Increased divorce rates

Increased number of women in the labor force

Rise in teenage pregnancy

Rise in school dropout rates

Changing cultural norms, such as an increasing social acceptance of having children out of wedlock

In addition to these economic and demographic factors that influence caseload size and potential budget savings, individual behavior greatly affects the responses AFDC clients have toward new federal policies. It is the individual who decides whether or not to apply for AFDC, whether or not to work, in which state she will live, and so forth. For example, the decision of whether or not to accept a job may be influenced by numerous motivational factors. A recipient is likely to consider any financial advantage or disadvantage from earnings, additional fringe benefits such as health care or life insurance, and the ability to get satisfactory and affordable child care. Psychological factors such as stress resulting from work, pride in working, boredom from not working, and opportunities for socializing may also directly affect the decision. Finally, stigma still plays an important part in the decision of work versus welfare because of the obvious negative societal connotation attached to the latter.

The result of all these problems with state data is that the information that became available in 1982–83 posed more questions than it resolved. For instance, the uneven pattern of terminations across states raised a question as to why the new provision counting stepparents' income was responsible for a majority of terminations in Georgia but for very few in other states. The question of how many terminated recipients returned to the rolls at a later time yielded a variety of different answers. Some states showed relatively low numbers of returnees, around 10 percent, while others estimated higher proportions at 20 and 30 percent.

In summary, state data were insufficient with which to draw any conclusions about the effects of specific provisions across states. The federal government recognized this and commissioned several studies specifically to assess OBRA's impact on AFDC families. These and other privately sponsored studies were necessary because of the states' inability to determine who was affected and how. In the end, it was up to the executive and congressional branches of the federal government—those who created the new law—to commission new research efforts to uncover the effects of their actions after the fact. Through these studies, we can get a little clearer sense of the results of OBRA than we can by looking to states for the information.

The research studies investigating the effects of OBRA were conducted between 1982 and 1984 by a variety of organizations, in different parts of the country, and with different methodologies. The largest of the studies was performed by the General Accounting Office (GAO) at the request of the House Ways and Means Committee, which has jurisdication over AFDC. Committee members were interested in determining the impact of the cuts on family income, lifestyles, and work effort. The Department of Health and Human Services, the federal executive agency responsible for AFDC, commissioned the Research Triangle Institute (RTI) to conduct a six-month study of, among other issues, how the policy changes affected recipients' work behavior. Later, the Congressional Research Service (CRS), an arm of Congress, asked Mathematica, Inc., to distinguish the effects of OBRA from the effects of the economic recession in 1981–82.

In addition to these government-sponsored studies, a host of privately funded studies were conducted by universities and research organizations. Among the major studies were the following:

The Institute for Research on Poverty at the University of Wisconsin assessed the effects of the budget cuts on Wisconsin AFDC families and published several reports.

The University of Minnesota conducted a similar study in Minnesota.

The Institute for Social Research at the University of Michigan, the School of Social Work at Columbia University, and the Center for the Study of Social Policy conducted a series of surveys of working AFDC recipients affected by the policy changes in Michigan, New York City, and Georgia.

Researchers and sponsors alike felt it was important to assess the impact of the AFDC policy changes. No one knew how these changes would affect the quality of life for those in poverty. While there had been some controversy regarding the work disincentive feature of the new policies, no one knew whether welfare recipients really would leave their jobs because they could receive as much money from not working. What was known was that the cuts represented a major departure from recent AFDC policy. But it was not self-evident, given the discretion maintained by state and local governments, what effects the new policies would have on work behavior.

The methodologies used in the studies varied considerably. Some relied on state budget and caseload data, others used computer simulations, and still others interviewed recipients in person or by phone. Despite different methodologies, the studies reached agreement on many points. And while some of the studies are not directly comparable, we summarize the findings below.

Budget and Caseload Reductions

Several studies sought to determine the effects of all the policy changes (not just those targeted on working recipients) on the program's costs and on the number of families receiving AFDC nationwide. In FY 1981, before OBRA was implemented, AFDC costs totaled $13.3 billion, of which federal dollars accounted for $7.15 billion, or slightly more than half. The Congressional Budget Office estimated that the 1981 policy changes would result in a $4.8 billion reduction in AFDC spending over FY 1982 to FY 1985,[1] representing a budget reduction of 12.7 percent over that period.[2] Using slightly different economic assumptions, the Urban Institute calculated that the cuts represented a 14.3 percent reduction in costs.[3] However, these figures do not account for increased AFDC costs due to clients who return to the rolls or increased costs in other related programs. As such, they may overstate the amount of savings resulting from OBRA.

Rather than estimating the effects over a three-year period, the General Accounting Office looked at actual caseload figures and concluded that immediately after the policy changes were implemented, AFDC spending was down by 9.3 percent in an average month.[4] The Congressional Research Service, using a computer model, attempted to account for the separate effects of the policy changes and the recession. CRS concluded that OBRA reduced AFDC spending by 13 percent but that the recession (which increased poverty) increased AFDC spending by 4 percent. Thus the net effect was an overall decrease of 9 percent in AFDC spending,[5] in line with GAO's findings. In sum, the AFDC policy changes would have reduced AFDC costs by approximately 13 to 14 percent but, because the recession added people to the rolls, the actual savings were closer to 9 percent.

There was also concurrence among the studies on the number of families who lost their AFDC benefits. Before OBRA, 3.7 million families received benefits. CBO estimated a total caseload reduction of nearly 10 percent for FY 1982–85. For FY 1982, GAO estimated a 13.7 percent reduction in the caseload, CRS estimated a 12 percent drop, and HHS calculated an 11.3 percent reduction.[6] Thus, it appears that between 10 and 13.7 percent of the total caseload (or 370,000 to 507,000 families) were dropped from the rolls nationwide.

Those who worked and received welfare—people the policies had sought to remove from the rolls—were more likely to lose eligibility than those who did not work. CBO found that half of the 500,000 AFDC families with earnings lost their benefits entirely, and another 40 percent, or 200,000 families, had them reduced. In comparison, approximately 100,000 nonworking families lost eligibility, and an equal number had their benefits reduced.[7] GAO found similar results. Examining a sample of case records in five cities, they discovered that from 40 to 60 percent of the working AFDC families had lost their eligibility and that another 8 to 48 percent had had their benefits reduced. In contrast, only 1 to 12 percent of the nonearner families were cut off the rolls, and only another

1 to 6 percent suffered reduced benefits.[8] These numbers represent the range of findings from the five sites.

In sum, the effects of the cuts on program costs and caseloads were not surprising; both were reduced around 12 percent on account of OBRA. The administration's goal to "wean" the working poor from the rolls was accomplished; most of those who lost AFDC benefits were working mothers.

However, a word about OBRA's alleged cost savings is necessary. The AFDC changes actually did relatively little to reduce federal costs when viewed in terms of the total federal budget, yet the money that was saved was targeted on a small number of recipients who had to absorb relatively large income losses.

Nationally, the federal government estimated that it would save approximately $1.2 billion in OBRA's first year as a result of all terminations and benefit reductions. Yet this was out of a total federal budget of $695 billion and out of $38 billion saved from all programs in FY 1982. Thus the relative contribution of savings from AFDC was minuscule in terms of the entire federal deficit.

The savings achieved were actually smaller than the administration had orginally sought. At least three factors were responsible for reducing the amount of savings that were actually produced. First, as noted in chapter 5, several states took actions to mitigate the effects of the new rules. These steps reduced cost savings. Second, if families return to AFDC because they leave their jobs, the benefits paid to them will be considerably higher than the supplemental benefits paid to them when they were working. That is, the family is likely to return to AFDC at a full grant rather than a partial grant, thereby reducing program savings.

Two states looked at the dollar offset created by higher grant cases coming back onto the rolls. Wisconsin found that of the $2.1 million in AFDC benefits paid prior to OBRA to families whose grants were later terminated or reduced, $1.3 million (62 percent) was spent on reopened cases. Although only 42.3 percent of Wisconsin's terminated cases had returned to the program, they did so at higher grant levels than when they were removed. Of the 3,934 cases closed from February through October 1982 because of the expiration of the $30 plus one-third disregard, 1,596 cases (41 percent) had reopened by mid-October 1982. A comparison of these families' grants in the month prior to termination with the grants received the first month after reopening indicates that the 1,596 reopened cases cost 86 percent as much as the 3,934 cases had cost prior to termination ($398,113 for 1,596 cases after reopening, compared with $465,089 for 3,934 cases prior to termination).

New York examined the income status of terminated recipients who returned to the rolls in comparison with their income status when they were first terminated. Of the 480 cases originally terminated because of the 150 percent cap who returned to the rolls within six months, only 16 percent had any earned income when they returned to the rolls. This is in contrast to 95 percent with earned income at the time of termination. Moreover, the average earnings for those reopened cases who had earned income was $385 per month, as opposed to $690 at the time of termination.[9] This suggests that the vast majority of people whose cases were reopened had either quit their jobs, lost them, or reduced their work effort. Thus, although the dollar figures associated with this phenomenon are not precise, it is clear that cost reductions claimed may not be realized when reopened cases are accounted for, many of which may be put back on the rolls at higher grant levels.

Third, savings generated by OBRA are offset by higher costs in other related programs. Food stamp costs for a family increase as AFDC benefits drop or cease; general assistance programs may have to pick up individuals and families terminated from AFDC; and a host of social service programs and public health-care programs may bear the brunt of trying to replace a family's lost income or lost Medicaid coverage. Several states reported that a ⌐ expansion in their General Assistance rolls may have been due at least in part to OBRA's AFDC terminations. For example, in Pennsylvania, the state General Assistance program rose by $35 million, or 11 percent, between July 1981 and July 1982. In New York, the General Assistance caseload rose by 25 percent and costs were up 30 percent. New York also collects data on the number of AFDC transfers to General Assistance. The number of these transfers rose by 94 percent between November 1981 and March 1982, the time period in which most of the AFDC terminations were made. A similar pattern of dollar offsets could well appear if data from public hospitals, emergency food pantries, and other social service/income support programs were available. Thus, one of OBRA's financial effects was to shift costs from the federal government to the states, or from one part of a state's budget to another.

It is therefore possible to calculate "lost" savings due to recipients returning to the rolls as well as higher costs in related programs. In fact, Wisconsin did this and found that, altogether, it lost 84 percent of the total OBRA-AFDC savings in the state. Of this total, 42 percent, or $13.5 million, was lost due to increased grants to recipients who returned to the rolls as shown earlier. Another $7.3 million was lost due to increased food stamps; because of the way food stamp benefits are calculated, for every dollar saved in AFDC, food stamps rose by $.30. Another $6 million was lost to the state treasury in taxes formerly paid by recipients with earnings. In total, $26.8 million in savings out of $32 million in potential savings was lost on account of these three factors.

So the OBRA changes may not have saved as much money as they were supposed to. States raised their need standards to offset some of the intended cuts; families returned to the rolls at higher grant levels; and some costs were merely shifted to other programs or levels of government. It must be remembered that AFDC is financed by both the federal government and state governments, so the federal savings of approximately $1.2 billion were only half the total savings; another $1.2 billion was allegedly saved by the states. Furthermore, the savings, small as they may have been, were concentrated on a group of recipients who, by virtue of their already low incomes, sorely felt the drop in income. When one gets to the level of individual families, the dollar reductions take on magnified value. Research on the effects of these cuts on individual families is reported below.

Impact on Families

The families affected by the new policies, most of whom worked, had very low incomes. Since AFDC eligibility limits vary from state to state, the income of families affected by the new policies also varied. Families in most sites had earnings below the national poverty level for a family of three. When the changes took effect, AFDC family earnings ranged from $450 a month in Georgia[10] and $562 in Dallas to $699 a month in Boston and $781 in Milwaukee.[11] In Georgia, more than four out of five of the sample of working families who lost all AFDC and Medicaid lived in poverty—even before the policies took effect.

Declining Income and Rising Poverty

The 1981 policy changes meant a complete loss of AFDC benefits for nearly half a million families. The amount of this loss for working families ranged from an average of $71 per month per family in Dallas to $198 per month per family in Milwaukee.[12]

Several studies also examined the AFDC loss for those working families who had their grants reduced but not eliminated entirely. As would be expected, the loss for these families was not as great. GAO found reductions ranging from $46 to $137, and those in Minnesota averaged $58.[13]

Faced with a sudden reduction in income, some of these parents were able to work longer hours and increase their earnings. Others qualified for increased food stamp allotments. These two factors helped some families reduce their losses under the new policies. Nevertheless, the average affected working family in the GAO sites lost from 12 to 31 percent of their total income.[14] Working recipients in Minnesota who lost AFDC lost 8 percent of their total income.

Losing AFDC benefits meant less income and more poverty for these families. In Georgia, the poverty rate among families increased from 81 to 88.5 percent, and in New York City, the proportion of the sample living below the poverty threshold increased from 28 to 52 percent.[15] The poverty rate among affected families in Wisconsin almost tripled—from 13.8 to 34.6 percent when all household income is counted.[16] In other words, more people were officially poor as a result of the AFDC cuts. At the same time, families already in poverty were pushed further below the poverty line.

Increasing Hardship

All of the studies found increasing hardship under the new policies—more hunger, larger debts, worsening medical care. GAO found that families had to borrow money more often and turned more often to food pantries and soup kitchens. One-third to one-half of affected families in Michigan, New York City, and Georgia ran completely out of food at least once; over 80 percent ran out of money; and one-third had bills more than two months overdue.[17] In Minnesota, 25 to 30 percent of the families affected by the new policies were either threatened with having their utilities shut off or actually had them shut off.[18]

The OBRA changes had serious detrimental effects on the health care of these families. Since AFDC eligibility automatically confers Medicaid eligibility, most of those who were terminated from AFDC also lost Medicaid coverage.

While some families obtained health insurance coverage through their employers, the studies found that many families were uninsured. Between 21 and 68 percent of the affected families lacked adequate health insurance. The consequences of the shortfall were severe: 14 to 24 percent of these families had forgone medical treatment because of the expense, and another 8 to 13 percent had been refused treatment because they lacked insurance.[19]

The most extensive investigation of the health care of these families was conducted in the Minnesota study. After losing Medicaid coverage, out-of-pocket medical expenses for these families quadrupled.[20] Thus, just as family income was being reduced, health expenses were increasing dramatically.

Family Responses to the Policy Changes

In general, the studies show that (1) the families slightly increased the number of hours worked, although not significantly, (2) the employment rate one year or more after OBRA remained very high, and (3) earnings increased even after inflation but far less than what would have been required to replace lost AFDC income.

GAO found that during the fall of 1983, between 63 and 88 percent of those who had been terminated from AFDC were employed. In Wisconsin, 91 percent of the terminees either were working at the same job or had found a new job. A year after termination, 85 percent of those in Minnesota were off AFDC and working. Since the unemployment rate for the overall population during this period was in the 10 percent range (with a great deal of local variation), the level of employment recorded here appears to be "normal."

After the policy changes, some families worked longer hours. One in six families in Boston and Syracuse increased their work hours, as did one in nine families in Memphis. In general, 11 to 16 percent of the families were able to increase their work hours.[21] Fourteen to 21 percent of the families terminated in Georgia, Michigan, and New York City were able to change jobs, increase their hours, or take an additional job.[22]

The GAO study found that family earnings increased in real terms but not enough to replace lost AFDC income. The increase in earnings varied greatly from site to site. Between the time they lost AFDC benefits and the time of interview (about one year later), families in Boston increased their earnings by an average of $176 a month; in Milwaukee the increase was $137. AFDC families in Minnesota increased their earnings by 10 percent.

The greatest controversy surrounding the new AFDC policies concerned their potential effect on the work behavior of these families. By removing the work-incentive provisions in AFDC, the new rules made it financially advantageous for many families to abandon work and subsist on welfare. Even if a family would have a slightly higher income by working that by not working, working meant the family would lose its Medicaid coverage. Because of this, some feared that the new rules would increase dependence.

Unfortunately, the most controversial question was also the most difficult one to answer. Researchers could measure how many families returned to the AFDC program after losing their benefits, but had difficulty determining whether the new rules actually changed this behavior.

The GAO study, for example, found that 11 to 30 percent of the families received AFDC during the year after they lost their benefits. The Institute for Research on Poverty (IRP) found that one-third of the families who lost benefits returned to AFDC in the following thirteen to seventeen months.[23] In Michigan, 24 percent of the sample returned to the rolls with 16 months; in New York City, 27 percent returned within

12 months, and 38 percent of the Georgia mothers came back on the rolls at some time within 19 months of being cut off AFDC.[24] But are these return rates "normal"? Did the new rules increase the number of families who stopped working and returned to AFDC?

To answer these questions, researchers needed to study a control group, a set of families who were similar to the families that lost benefits but who were not affected by the new rules. Since the new regulations applied to all states, it was impossible to find working AFDC families not affected by the new rules. Therefore, any control group is severely limited. Faced with this predicament, two studies used data from an earlier period as a control group. The GAO and Research Triangle studies used welfare case records from an earlier year to determine the so-called normal return rate. They then compared this rate to the rate observed among the families that lost benefits as a result of OBRA. RTI found no change in the return rate; GAO found that the return rate among families who lost benefits under OBRA was lower than the return rate in the control group.[25]

There are some problems with this approach. First, the families who lost benefits under OBRA could not be directly compared to the families from earlier periods. Control groups consisted of all working AFDC families, while the families affected by OBRA had unique characteristics: because they were affected by the new OBRA rules, they had higher wages than other earners on AFDC; they may have had higher work expenses; and they may have had a stronger attachment to the workforce. Thus the control groups cannot have been directly comparable with those terminated on account of OBRA. At best, the control group can be only an approximation.

Moreover, it is likely that the return rate is affected by macroeconomic changes—higher unemployment in an area might mean a higher return rate to AFDC. Comparing groups of families from two different time periods does not account for this difference.

Nevertheless, both the RTI and the GAO studies concluded that recipients had not quit work. The administration touted these findings as evidence of the success of its policies. Yet should one congratulate oneself that AFDC mothers chose not to quit their jobs even though their disposable income is not comparable to that of nonworking families?

There are at least two reasons we should not be surprised by these findings. First, financial incentives such as those used in AFDC are by no means the only determinant of work behavior. Economists have recognized this fact for years. People choose to work or not on the basis of many considerations, only one of which is financial remuneration. Jobs carry with them self-esteem, a sense of pride in one's accomplishment. For many of the women interviewed in Georgia, a job was a way to get out of the house and keep from "going crazy" sitting home. Thus, many of the mothers may have chosen to keep their jobs for reasons other than the financial reward.

Second, the financial rewards resulting from the AFDC work-incentive provisions have never been substantial. The work-incentive disregard added to the system in 1967 was only worth $30 plus one-third of the remaining earnings. This was not a large sum then and it has never been indexed since it was first enacted, so it is worth even less today. Social policy analysts have known for years that the work-incentive provisions are only marginal in value. Still, they believed it was important to have policy reflect the principle that working families should have more money than nonworking families—even if that meant in practice only a very little more money. So again, it is not surprising that AFDC mothers did not quit their jobs. But that in no way exonerates policymakers for removing the principle of a work incentive.

In summary, each of the findings reported in this chapter must be viewed with caution. None of the studies could be controlled experiments and even those that used approximate control groups could not exactly match the experimental group. Additionally, the dynamic nature of the AFDC caseload and the confounding effects of the economy limit the findings even further. Nevertheless, the results of the studies collectively show that as a result of OBRA, many families were cut off AFDC, primarily those with earnings. Research efforts focused primarily on earners have found that, contrary to popular impression, these people were not well off at the time of the cuts, which significantly decreased their income and increased destitution. Although the evidence indicates that the effort was made, private earnings could not come close to making up for the income losses due to reduced or terminated AFDC grants. And in spite of a lessened incentive to work, OBRA does not appear to have decreased work effort.

Policy Implications

The focus on recidivism put researchers in an awkward position. The issue, which had become central to the policy debate, was almost impossible to address adequately, since a comparable control group was impossible to secure. For researchers, keeping their work "policy relevant" meant straining the limits of research.

This illustrates a larger problem in policy research today. Too often, research is detached from the policy-making dialogue. Even when it is related to a specific policy decision, research findings often are not timely for purposes of making policy decisions. Too often, researchers are re-actors rather than actors, responding ex post facto to policies and re-sponding within a political context. The political debate clearly shaped and narrowed the studies of the OBRA policies: study after study showed the anticipated losses, but few, if any, considered more broadly the plight of low-income workers or related findings to alternative policies that promised to better meet these families' needs.

This is not to denigrate the usefulness of these studies. Without them we would know nothing of the human impact of the new policies. Through them, we see something of the human dimension of the policy changes: how families coped with the income and Medicaid losses. A more detailed look at the families in one of the studies is presented in the next chapter.

Notes

1. Congressional Budget Office, *Major Legislative Changes in Human Resources Program Since January 1981,* August 1983, vii.

2. Ibid., 34.

3. Urban Institute, *The Reagan Record* (Cambridge, Massachusetts: Ballinger, 1984), 185.

4. General Accounting Office, *An Evaluation of the 1981 AFDC Changes: Initial Analysis,* 2 April 1984, 4.

5. Congressional Research Service, *Effects of the Omnibus Budget Reconciliation Act of 1984 (OBRA) Welfare Changes and the Recession on Poverty,* 25 July 1984, 3.

6. House Committee on Ways and Means, *Background Material and Data on Programs Within the Jurisdiction of the Committee on Ways and Means,* 21 February 1984, 324.

7. Congressional Budget Office, *Major Legislative Changes,* 39.

8. General Accounting Office, *Evaluation of AFDC Changes,* 4.

9. Office of Program Planning, Analysis and Development, New York State Department of Social Services, "Effects of Selected Program Changes on Public Assistance and Food Stamp Cases from January through July 1982," March 1983.

10. Center for the Study of Social Policy, *Working Female-Headed Families in Poverty: Three Studies of Low-Income Families Affected by the AFDC Policy Changes of 1981,* March 1984.

11. General Accounting Office, *Evaluation of AFDC Changes,* 48.

12. Ibid., 4.

13. Center for Health Services Research, Center for Urban and Regional Affairs, the University of Minnesota, *The Impact of Federal Cutbacks on Working AFDC Recipients in Minnesota,* December 1983, 22.

14. General Accounting Office, *Evaluation of AFDC Changes,* 48.

15. Center for the Study of Social Policy, *Working Female-Headed Families in Poverty,* ii.

16. Institute for Research on Poverty, *Poverty and Welfare Recipiency in Wisconsin After OBRA,* Discussion Paper, 1985.

17. Center for the Study of Social Policy, *Working Female-Headed Families in Poverty,* 67–68.

18. Center for Health Services Research, University of Minnesota, *Impact of Federal Cutbacks,* ii.

19. General Accounting Office, *Evaluation of AFDC Changes,* 41, and Center for the Study of Social Policy, *Working Female-Headed Families in Poverty,* 73.

20. Center for Health Services Research, University of Minnesota, *Impact of Federal Cutbacks,* 23.

21. General Accounting Office, *Evaluation of AFDC Changes,* 47.

22. Center for the Study of Social Policy, *Working Female-Headed Families in Poverty,* 58.

23. Institute for Research on Poverty, *Poverty and Welfare Recipiency,* 6.

24. Center for the Study of Social Policy, *Working Female-Headed Families in Poverty,* ii.

25. Research Triangle Institute, *Evaluation of the 1981 AFDC Amendments,* Final Report, 15 April 1983.

8
Effects on Working Families in Georgia

*J*anuary 1977: Valerie Branch returns to Georgia from her sister's in Indiana and receives the final divorce papers from her husband's lawyer. Having looked for work for almost a year, she finally finds a job as a housekeeper at a local motel. Valerie also receives partial AFDC payments.

> They paid me $3.35 an hour, but I never made a 40-hour week. It was usually five hours a day, or five and one-half, sometimes four days one week then maybe five days the next week. But then they started cutting back on the hours more. The business got slow and they just couldn't carry more, so they let me go.

May 1978: Valerie receives $48 per week in unemployment compensation while she looks for another job. Three months later she gets a job as a dishwasher in a local restaurant, again making minimum wage and getting some AFDC. Valerie complains about the working conditions, although she stays at the job for three years.

> If somebody takes sick and couldn't come in, they get angry and threaten to fire you. You can really be sick and they want you to come in and work anyway. And we be in the kitchen where it's so hot from noon to 8:00. The waitresses get to eat in the dining room but us kitchen help have to eat in the kitchen.

> One day the boss comes in and tells this lady next to me to go out there and clean up the trash. The waitresses had sat their trash down on the side of the dumpster and the dogs came along and tore it all up. Well, it was so hot the maggots had got in and we had to clean it up. Sometimes I wondered if that job was worth it for $3.35 an hour.

August 1982: Valerie is fired from the restaurant when her boss accuses her of stealing a bowl of tuna salad. Valerie maintains she wasn't stealing it because the boss's wife had told her to throw it out.

We had tuna that Thursday, and I asked the boss's wife what do you want me to do with this because sometimes they would take the tuna salad and save it and serve it the next day. She said, "Well get rid of it," so I told the other girl, "I'm not going to throw this in the trash because it's still good. I'm going to carry it home to my kids." So that is what I did, I wrapped it in aluminum foil and put it in my purse.

February 1983: Valerie has not been able to find another job. She reflects on the future:

These jobs that pay $3.35 an hour just aren't enough; when they get through taking out the taxes on you, you don't have nothing to bring home. I need some kind of career. I need a job that pays decent wages so I can provide for my three kids.

When the administration announced its 1981 budget cuts in AFDC, it asserted that the families being cut were not families in poverty but rather families who could make it on their own, without public assistance. The administration contended that families who lost benefits were families with enough income to support themselves. Indeed, President Reagan stated in a news conference on April 4, 1984, that the families removed from the AFDC rolls "were families that had considerable outside earnings."[1]

Yet this was not an accurate assessment, according to data from a survey of working recipients in Georgia. Of the working families who were cut off the rolls, a sample of 207 were interviewed and their case records reviewed to assess the impact of the cuts. The focus of this study was the working families who had their AFDC grants terminated as opposed to those who were cut from the rolls on account of other OBRA provisions.

All the families in the survey were headed by single women, and all the women had been working when their aid was terminated. Seventy-nine percent were black and 21 percent were white. The average family was made up of a mother and 2 children. Half of the families lived in extended households with other adults, usually the mother's parents or siblings. The remainder lived alone, that is, the mother and her children lived by themselves. A total of 849 persons lived in the households of these families: in addition to the 207 mothers and their 422 children, there were another 144 adults and 76 other children (usually nieces and nephews) who lived in the extended households.

Many of the families lived in larger households in order to minimize their expenses. It was not uncommon to find a mother and two children living in an extended family with her own mother and brother and sister and several nieces and nephews, all in a small three-bedroom house.

The women were generally in their late twenties. The children ranged in age from less than one year to twenty-one, with a median age of nine. Over a third of the children were under age five, and most of the school-age children were in school.

All the mothers in the sample had been working; in fact, most of them had been working steadily. Half worked for at least twenty-one out of the twenty-seven months between Sepatember 1980 and November 1982, an overall weak period in the U.S. economy. Almost all had worked for at least twelve months out of that period.

Generally, the women held nontechnical, nonmanagerial positions. Virtually all (95 percent) of the women in the study were service workers, factory operatives, or clerical workers.

Table 8–1 provides a better sense of the employment of these women. It is a random list of some of the jobs, hours, and salaries of the women in the study. Some of the women worked in restaurants as cooks, waitresses, or dishwashers, sometimes working the 11 P.M. to 7 A.M. shift in all-night restaurants. Many worked as housekeepers, either in private homes or motels (usually from 8:30 A.M. to 2:30 P.M. three or four days a week) and earned about $55 a week after taxes. Several worked as office cleaners from 5:30 to 8:30 P.M., five nights a week. Most of the women in clerical positions (mail clerks, sales clerks, and clerk typists, for example) worked regular hours from 8:00 A.M. to 4:30 P.M. and brought home about $120 each week. Finally, some of the women worked in factories as seamstresses, clothes pressers, or clothes cleaners. These women earned less than $200 per week after taxes.

These jobs constitute what is sometimes called the "secondary labor market." Virtually all of the women (79 percent) were paid by the hour; 6 percent were paid on a piecework basis that often fluctuated. Moreover, the wages were low. One-fifth of the jobs paid $3.00 or less per hour; half paid between $3.00 and $4.00 per hour. Only 10 percent of the jobs paid more than $5.00 per hour.

Few of the women were self-employed, although two had converted their homes into day-care centers. Only 7 percent of the women worked at jobs covered by a union contract, and only half of these women belonged to the union. Thus, few of them had the benefit of a union working on their behalf for greater pay, better benefits, and/or better working conditions. The fringe benefits provided to these women were minimal. Only 32 percent had health and hospital insurance provided by their employer for themselves and their children; 41 percent received paid sick leave; and two-thirds received paid vacation.

Many of the women had had hopes for better jobs than they now hold. For example, one woman had received a secretarial degree from a technical school but is now an office clerk for a soft-drink distributor.

Table 8–1
Examples of Jobs, Time Worked, and Pay

	Hours	Number of Days Per Week	Number of Hours Per Week	Pay Per Week
Food-service assistant at school	7:30 a.m.–4:00 p.m.	5	40	$125 after taxes
Cashier at Krystal Hamburgers	11:00 p.m.–7:00 p.m.	5	40	$115 after taxes
Seamstress in dress shop	8:00 a.m.–4:30 p.m.	5	40	$215 before taxes
Waitress	5:00 a.m.–5:00 p.m.	6	72	$2/hour plus tips
Machinist at factory that makes bumper cars	7:00 a.m.–4:00 p.m.	5	40	$200 before taxes
Clothes presser	8:00 a.m.–4:30 p.m.	5	40	$120 after taxes
Cleaning coats for clothes manufacturer	8:00 a.m.–4:30 p.m.	5	40	$217 after taxes
Data transcriber for IRS	3:00 p.m.–11:00 p.m.	5	40	$220 before taxes
Sales clerk at drugstore	7:00 a.m.–3:30 p.m.	5	40	$100 after taxes
Housekeeping aide at hospital	8:00 a.m.–4:30 p.m.	4	32	$150 after taxes
Mail clerk at jewelry wholesalers	5:00 p.m.–8:00 p.m.	5	22	$110 after taxes
Nursery attendant at bowling alley	10:30 a.m.–7:00 p.m.	6	40	$73 before taxes
Food-service aide at hospital	8:00 a.m.–3:00 p.m.	5	27	$150 after taxes
Cashier at Burger King	Rotating shifts	5	32	$75 after taxes
Cook at Church's Fried Chicken				$132 after taxes
Office clerk for soft-drink distributor	9:30 a.m.–4:00 p.m.	5	32	$152 before taxes
Peeling machine operator at shrimp company	6:30 a.m.–2:00 p.m.	4	28	$68 after taxes
Housekeeper in private home	8:30 a.m.–2:30 p.m.	3	20	$55 after taxes
Cook at Waffle House	5:30 p.m.–9:00 p.m.	6	20	$40 after taxes
Office cleaner	5:30 a.m.–8:30 p.m.	5	15	$50 before taxes
Photocopy clerk in university library	8:00 a.m.–5:00 p.m.	5	40	$149 after taxes
Clerk typist for clothing warehouse	9:00 a.m.–5:00 p.m.	5	38	$137 after taxes
Housekeeping aide in nursing home	9:00 a.m.–5:00 p.m.	5	40	$107 after taxes
Dishwasher in bakery	8:00 a.m.–3:00 p.m.	6	44	$115 before taxes

Source: "Coping with Poverty: Working-Poor Families in Georgia." The Center for the Study of Social Policy, Washington, D.C., July 1984.

Another woman had attended a vocational school in commercial art, hoping to be a window dresser or to work in design advertising. That was ten years ago; now she is a clerk-typist for a clothing warehouse. Still another woman had been going to a junior college and taking nursing preparatory courses but is now a nurse's aide. She admitted that while she would like to be a nurse, "I know I am not qualified for what I want to do." And another remarked, "I go to look for a better job and they say 'no.' Maybe I'm not dressed properly or they don't like my teeth. Whatever it is, I am not what they are looking for." This woman now cleans offices each evening for a paycheck of less than $45 per week.

The women in this study worked in spite of the fact that many had health problems or had to care for children with health problems. During 1982, 55 percent of the families in the study had four or more conditions of poor health. Fifty-two percent had a child under age six and not yet in school. Although AFDC allows these mothers to stay home with their young children, each chose to work instead.

The sense of dedication to the work ethic can be seen as clearly in the women's responses to questions about work. Almost all the women reported that they liked their jobs. Two-thirds wanted to work more hours, in spite of the fact that half were already working full-time. Many noted that they felt a need to be self-supporting or independent—a feeling that comes with working. Others indicated that working provides an opportunity to improve their lives, noting that they have "more of a future with a job." Finally, many of the women mentioned they were embarrassed to be on welfare and much preferred work whenever they could find it.

Preference for work was consistently expressed despite the fact that it meant the mothers could not spend much time with their children. They chose to work even though many believed it would have been better for their children if they could have stayed home to care for them.

The picture that emerges is one of hard-working women trying to better their own and their children's lives through work. There are many reasons these women could justify staying home, among them poor health or being needed at home to raise their young children. Yet they persist in the labor market, working long hours in low-paying jobs with often few or no benefits, and often with very little chance for advancement in their jobs.

The Budget Cuts

The administration's assertions that OBRA removed only families with considerable earnings fails to account for the interstate variation in AFDC eligibility and benefit levels. In Georgia, where payments are among the lowest nationwide, children and working mothers with very low wages were cut from the program. Although the women in this study were the highest earners among all working women on welfare in Georgia, their earnings, at 75 percent of poverty, could hardly be called adequate, considering the costs of raising a family today.

Table 8–2 shows the earnings levels for the women in the sample when their welfare benefits were terminated. Overall, the average gross earnings for the families were $447 per month. At full-time work this translates into $2.58 per hour, or 77 percent of the minimum wage. Forty-two percent of the entire sample earned less than $400 per month, and 87 percent had gross incomes of less than $600 per month. Thus, the new rules responsible for terminating working women in Georgia took their toll on mothers who were trying to raise their families on gross earnings of $447 monthly, or about $393 in take-home pay.

Most of the women in the study later reported that they were bewildered when they received notice that their welfare check would be terminated. They knew only that new federal rules meant that their earned income was now too high to qualify for aid. Yet they wondered how the government could think that their earnings were enough to live on, when it knew they already had difficulty providing food, clothing, and shelter for their children on their earnings alone. In this sense, the gulf between Washington, D.C., and Georgia seemed enormous.

Phoebe Dellums is a rather talkative women, full of colorful stories that she tells with a flair and illustrates with an expressive face. She lives and works in Savannah, earning about $400 a month in a fast-food restaurant. In September 1980, her earnings, which must support Phoebe and her three children, were supplemented by $122 in food stamps and $148 in AFDC.

Table 8–2
Monthly Earnings at Termination

Earnings	Families
0–$200	1
$201–$400	86 (42%)
$401–$600	93 (45%)
$601–$800	26 (13%)
$801 +	1
Average $447 (77% of full-time minimum wage)	

Source: "Coping with Poverty: Working-Poor Families in Georgia." The Center for the Study of Social Policy, Washington, D.C., July 1984.

. . . It's hard out there. You might get a job that makes $3.35 . . . but you hardly have anything to bring home. You can barely feed your kids.

. . . I think a mother that has three children, that lives in a house that costs $175 a month and my light bill built up to $143, and my gas bill is still in the $200's . . . I think they should give a mother that got kids enough money to pay her bills. To make sure her bills is paid, so the kids will have somewhere to stay.

In October 1981, under the policy changes of OBRA, Phoebe no longer qualified for assistance. Her monthly income dropped from about $670 to $520. She also lost her Medicaid coverage.

Being as money is very limited, I'd much prefer to see my children with things than me. I'll just do without. After the rent and my bills—and you know those food stamps don't last but three weeks when I stretch—there's nothing left for anything like clothes or even school supplies for the kids. They have to borrow from other kids . . . I'll be lucky if I can buy paper and pencils for them once a month.

As shown in chapter 5, Georgia was one of several states that chose to increase its need standard as a direct result of the new federal cap so that fewer working-poor AFDC recipients would have their aid cut off. This action was taken as a way of avoiding terminations while not increasing payments. Because Georgia kept its payment level the same and only raised its need standard, it did not have to pay families more money; rather, it merely enabled more working families to stay on the rolls. In this respect, the Georgia legislature and executive branch were willing to forgo some of the short-term cost savings promised from the federal cuts because they did not wish to eliminate aid to low-income working mothers and their children. Between August 1981, when it became known that new federal rules would cut working recipients whose incomes exceeded 150 percent of the need standard, and October 1981, when the law took effect, Georgia raised its need standard by 90 percent, almost doubling it. In July 1981, the need standard for a three-person family was $193; the governor, the Human Resources Department, and both chambers of the legislature quickly became concerned that the new 150 percent cap would terminate some 15,000 Georgia families, or half of all working families in the state. The state leaders wished to continue assistance to families at the margin, those trying to pull themselves out of poverty by working. They also knew that the new rule, which would most importantly cut Medicaid for these families, would tighten fiscal constraints on county hospitals that would no longer be able to get Medicaid reimbursement for these indigent families. The state leaders realized that the aid paid to working families was so small that it was worth the cost.

As a result, the Board of Human Resources increased the state need standard to $366 for a family of three, effective October 1, 1981. If Georgia had not raised its need standard, all three-person families with gross incomes over $289.50 per month (150 percent of $193) would have lost their AFDC benefits. By raising the standard, the cap terminated only three-person families with monthly incomes above $549.

Impact of the Cuts

Figure 8–1 shows the effects of the OBRA policy changes on the average family's income in the study. Without the cuts, average monthly income, comprised of gross earnings, AFDC, and food stamps, was $609. When the cuts took effect, the AFDC grant was reduced from $64 to zero and the average food stamp allotment rose slightly, but total monthly income declined by 10 percent, to $554.

The reduction of monthly income does not reflect the loss of Medicaid, which was in many ways more significant than the loss of the AFDC payment. One woman noted, "The only thing I really missed is Medicaid. They encourage you to work, but now I can't afford to take my kids to the doctor."

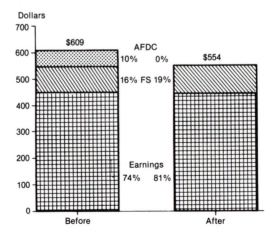

Source: "Coping with Poverty: Working-Poor Families in Georgia." The Center for the Study of Social Policy, Washington, D.C., July 1984.

Figure 8–1. Monthly Income before and after OBRA

In Georgia, Medicaid expenditures averaged $980 in health care per adult per year and $380 per child per year for those who used Medicaid.[2] Once this health coverage was eliminated, mothers had to find other means of paying for health care, do without it, or incur medical debts. As we will see later, many of the mothers either had to do without medical care or built up large medical debts.

In addition to losing Medicaid, some of the families also became ineligible for food stamps when they lost their AFDC benefits. For some, new restrictions on eligibility for food stamps may have been the reason. But for others, food stamps should not have been cut off. One explanation based on several cases we reviewed is that some counties automatically eliminated benefits to these families as "AFDC-plus-food-stamp" cases, notifying the families that they would have to reapply as "food-stamp-only" cases, and the families, not understanding this, or for some other reason, failed to reapply for food stamps.

Most families, however, had their food stamps increased slightly when their AFDC grant was eliminated. When AFDC benefits decrease, food stamp allotments automatically rise, although not enough to compensate for the AFDC drop. However, at the same time the federal budget cuts took effect in AFDC, cuts were made in the food stamp program as well. The net result of these changes was a small food stamp increase for the families in the sample. For these families, the average increase in food stamps was $9 per month, when their earnings were held constant. This $9 gain, however, was hardly enough to compensate for the $64 monthly AFDC loss.

The financial impact of OBRA on these families can also be measured using the national poverty threshold, which is designed to gauge a bare subsistence-level income. Before OBRA took effect, 81 percent of the families in the study lived below the official poverty line. OBRA both increased the number of poor families and also pressed already poor families deeper into poverty; after OBRA, 89 percent of the sample lived in poverty (see table 8–3).

The effect of the cuts was most noticeable at the lower end of the poverty scale. The OBRA budget cuts quadrupled the number of families living below 50 percent of the poverty threshold, which amounts to about $321 per month for a family of three. Even using "alternative income concepts," which include noncash benefits such as food stamps, OBRA deepened poverty among working single mothers in Georgia (see figures 8–2 and 8–3).

Louise Blanche and her two children, aged nine and twelve, live in a small rented house. The house has two bedrooms, a living room, kitchen, and bathroom, but it is badly in need of repair and paint on the outside.

Table 8–3
Poverty Rates before and after the Federal Cuts

	Without Food Stamps		With Food Stamps	
Percent of Poverty	Before	After	Before	After
>150%	1%	0%	2%	0.5%
126%–150%	4%	1.5%	6%	3.5%
101%–125%	14%	10%	22%	17%
76%–100%	29%	25%	52%	43%
51%– 75%	46%	40%	18%	32%
26%– 50%	6%	23%	0%	4%
< 25%	0%	0.5%	0%	0%
Average monthly income	$512	$449	$609	$554

Source: "Coping with Poverty: Working-Poor Families in Georgia." The Center for Study of Social Policy, Washington, D.C., July 1984.

While neat on the inside, flies are everywhere since there are no screens on the windows.

Louise has worked for the past six years cleaning rooms in a motel in downtown Athens. She works from 7:00 A.M. to 2:30 P.M. six days a week and brings home anywhere from $50 to $110 per week (she gets $1.50 for every room she cleans). When her monthly AFDC check of

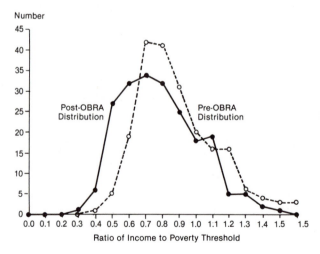

Source: "Coping with Poverty: Working-Poor Families in Georgia." The Center for the Study of Social Policy, Washington, D.C., July 1984.

Figure 8–2. Income Distribution Pre- and Post-OBRA Monthly Cash Income Only

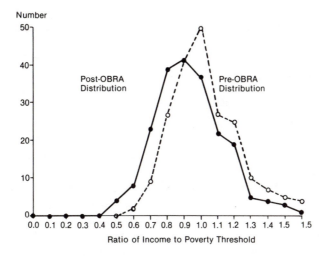

Source: "Coping with Poverty: Working-Poor Families in Georgia." The Center for the Study of Social Policy, Washington, D.C., July 1984.

Figure 8–3. Income Distribution Pre- and Post-OBRA Monthly Cash and Food Stamp Income

$68 and her Medicaid coverage were canceled, Louise felt the effects directly.

> I still brought home the same paycheck but had to stretch it further. Except for food, I had to pay all my bills out of my paychecks [about $360 per month]. I pay $225 in rent and my electricity, gas and phone bills are around $75 altogether. Then I got to pay my neighbor $2 a day to drive me to work. That leaves me about $5 a week to buy cleaning supplies, toilet paper, toothpaste, lightbulbs, school supplies, and so on.

When Louise's son Tyrone fell through a glass door and needed emergency medical treatment, she didn't know how she would pay for it.

> Every month since the accident, I get a notice from the hospital saying I'm past due on my bill for $576. And every month I know I'm not going to be able to pay it. I only hope they won't turn me away if my kids ever need emergency care again.

Reflecting on the effects of her AFDC loss on her family's well-being, Louise notes:

Things are worse, a lot worse now. I ain't ever been down as low as I am now. It'll be a hard time to keep going if something don't change.

The Loss of Work Incentives

The AFDC policy changes in OBRA had costs beyond those measured in family income. OBRA effectively eliminated the work-incentive provisions incorporated into AFDC in 1967. These provisions had been designed to ensure that working families were financially better off than nonworking families.

Under OBRA, many families with a working mother actually had less disposable income than those with a nonworking mother. After the budget cuts took effect, the average family in the study had an income of $554 ($446 in earnings and $108 in food stamps). Subtracting payroll and income taxes ($45) as well as average work and child-care expenses ($120 per month) left the working family with a disposable monthly income of $389. In the same month, a nonworking mother and her two children would receive $183 in AFDC and $199 in food stamps for a total income of $382, or only $7 less than the working family. Thus, the mother who worked full-time at thirty-five hours per week brought home 20 cents an hour more than the nonworking mother. Moreover, a family with slightly above-average work or child-care expenses or one with slightly below-average earnings would actually have less disposable income than would a nonworking family.

Even more important, the nonworking mother would have Medicaid coverage for herself and her children. As noted above, only about one-third of the women had insurance coverage comparable to Medicaid through their employers. For those uninsured, working was almost certainly less financially advantageous than not working.

Janice Tripp and her daughter Vanessa, aged seven, had their welfare grant of $40 per month terminated in October 1981. Janice was working as a receptionist in the county health clinic thirty-five hours a week for $3.35 an hour. She also had a Medicaid card for Vanessa and herself.

When I was working it made me feel good inside even though they were still giving me my welfare check, because while I was working, I still felt independent. I thought that they felt that I was independent enough to get out there and try to better myself and that's why they were still helping me. But then they cut me off, just like that. I really didn't want to quit my job, but I thought about reducing my hours so I could get my Medicaid card back. But I realized I just wouldn't make it either way.

Much controversy has surrounded the possible impact of the work disincentive established under OBRA on the work behavior of AFDC recipients. Irrespective of the behavioral impact, we have already seen the severe financial hardships that the loss of AFDC and Medicaid posed for these families. Equally important is the more elusive attitudinal value of work incentives: low-income working recipients often see assistance as commending their work effort. Throughout our study, women expressed some sense of abandonment by government: the dollars they had received not only helped meet basic needs but also symbolized society's approval of their work effort. The removal of this intangible benefit, while not quantifiable, is certainly significant.

Responses to the Losses

Faced with termination of aid, the mothers had few if any opportunities to make up for the loss. Twenty percent asked their child(ren)'s father for more child support; however, most reported they were unsuccessful at getting more help from the father. Fifteen percent moved from where they were living at the time; most of these moved in with others, usually back with their parents, or into a cheaper apartment or house. For example, one woman, when terminated from AFDC, took her two children and moved back in with her parents. After five months, she was able to move out into an apartment with one of her girlfriends but she could not afford to bring her three- and four-year-old children with her. They have remained with their grandparents.

Another woman reported that she had had to move four times since her termination: first, she and her child moved in with a roommate to share expenses, but she still couldn't afford the rent; then she accepted a live-in housekeeping job which covered the rent, but that did not work out; third, she and her child moved back in with her mother; and only twelve months later, when she got a new job, was she able once again to move out on her own.

Only a very few women (7 percent) went back to school or started a job training program. Most reported they could not afford to go back to school when tuition and child-care costs were considered.

Only 12 percent of the women were able to offset some of the AFDC loss by increasing their earnings; these mothers were the lucky ones who were able to increase the hours they worked or take an additional job (see table 8–4). For example, one mother took an additional job bartendering for the American Legion; another began selling Avon cosmetics on the side to try to make more money. Several mothers mentioned that

Table 8–4
Employment Changes Immediately after Termination

Employment Change	Percent of Sample
Hours reduced by employer	1.9%
Reduced hours voluntarily	0%
Changed jobs	2.4%
Increased hours	10.1%
Took additional job	1.9%
Laid off, quit, fired	1.0%
Other	1.0%
No change	81.2%

Source: "Coping with Poverty: Working-Poor Families in Georgia." The Center for the Study of Social Policy, Washington, D.C., July 1984.

while they thought about taking another job, they felt they could not pay for the increased child care they would need.

Most of the mothers had to try to make ends meet on less money. Because they had had no "padding" or luxuries in their budgets before the cuts, and because most were not able to compensate for the lost income, they had to reduce their monthly expenses, and this often came out of basic necessities.

A number of the mothers reported that the AFDC cut adversely affected their ability to pay for child care while they worked. Twenty-two percent were forced to make some changes in their child-care arrangement or payment. Eight percent had to take their child(ren) out of the supervised day-care center or nursery school because they could no longer afford it. Some of these mothers now had to take their child(ren) to work with them, let them stay alone (when the children were ten, eleven, or twelve), or find some other less expensive form of care. Several mothers, for instance, had to take their children to a relative's house, sometimes out of town.

Five percent of the mothers worked out new arrangements with their babysitters such that they paid the sitter less or used the sitter for fewer hours. Nine percent of the sample reported that they had to forfeit other basic expenses in order to pay for child care out of their earnings, since AFDC had previously paid for their child care through a special child-care allowance for working mothers.

Eventually, almost half of these families reapplied for aid. Some reapplied because they were working less or not at all, because they could not earn enough on their own to meet their basic expenses, or because they needed Medicaid. Another 31 percent of the mothers felt they needed to reapply for aid but did not do so because they thought they would be ineligible, there was too much red tape involved, or they did not want to be on welfare because of the stigma.

While half of the women reapplied for aid, 38 percent were reinstated within nineteen months. Almost all the mothers who came back on AFDC were not working at the time they came back on. These mothers had either lost their jobs by being laid off or fired, or they quit voluntarily. The remainder of the women who came back on AFDC, while they were still working, had lower earnings than when they had been terminated, presumably because their employers or they themselves had reduced the number of hours they worked.

Each of the mothers who came back on AFDC did so at a higher grant level than she had been on when her grant was eliminated. The average AFDC grant before termination was $64, while the average grant upon return for those who came back on the rolls was $164. Thus, on average, the seventy-nine women who came back on AFDC after being terminated received $100 more in AFDC than they had before their termination.

Because of the higher grants upon return, much of the intended cost savings of the AFDC cuts may not have materialized. Data from the study indicate that the cost savings resulting from four AFDC terminations would be offset by a single family's coming back on AFDC when food stamp costs are also included. Consider the following example.

The average Georgia AFDC family lost $64 in AFDC and gained $9 in food stamps, for a net program savings of $55. However, a family who came back on AFDC with no earnings cost the government $233 ($164 in AFDC and $69 more in food stamps). Thus, the return of a single family in Georgia at a cost to the government of $233 would more than offset the savings from the termination of four families ($55 × 4 = $220).

In summary, the women were not able to make up for the lost AFDC through their earnings. Only a very few were lucky enough to find better jobs or increase their hours at work. As a result, half reapplied for aid. Thirty-eight percent came back on AFDC at some point between the time they were cut off and July 1983, thereby negating much of the intended cost savings.

Making Ends Meet One to Two Years Later

Kathryn Locke and her two teenage sons live with her mother and brother in a house outside Jefferson. Kathryn's mother has a bad heart and can no longer work. Her brother was laid off from a construction job ten months ago.

> So we was all living off one paycheck: mine. And that was only $185 every two weeks. Plus we had the stamps for food.

Kathryn couldn't stretch her paycheck to meet all the mortgage payments on her mother's house, and soon found herself five months behind. She received a notice that they would be evicted if they didn't pay immediately. Kathryn borrowed $800 from a finance company to pay the mortgage debt. Now she doesn't know how she's going to repay the finance company at their high interest rates.

> It's not that I don't budget. I stretch to make every penny count. The kids don't get to go places and I'm always having problems keeping them in clothes. Just going to the laundry is expensive. It seems like prices keep going up and up but my income don't. I tell you, it puts a lot of worry on me.

In general, the families interviewed eighteen months after being cut off welfare could not make ends meet. Their average monthly income was $400 to $600, primarily from earnings and food stamps, although some had come back on AFDC. (A few had married or found boyfriends and were substantially better off, with an average additional income of $721 per month. These women were no longer on AFDC.)

For each dollar of income, the families averaged $1.18 in expenses. Despite the fact that children in 81 percent of the families received free school lunches, food expenses were high, consuming 40 percent of the family budget. The families spent 23 percent of their income on housing, which was largely small single-family houses or apartments. One-third of the families lived in government-subsidized housing. Approximately two out of three families rented, paying on average $100 per month; 13 percent owned their own home, paying an average mortgage of $156 per month; and the remainder lived with their parents or other relatives or in government housing, and paid little or no rent (see figure 8–4).

Child-care costs consumed 13 percent of the families' incomes. The mothers generally used friends and relatives to care for their children, and most paid nothing for this care. Almost three-quarters of the mothers who used child care relied on friends and relatives. These informal arrangements were far less costly than day-care centers, which were used by only 17 percent of the mothers with young children. Only one in five mothers who used child care paid for it, spending an average of $60 per month.

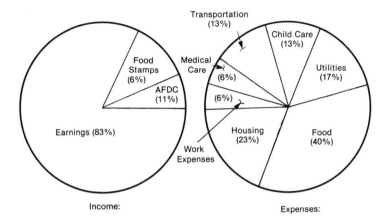

Income: Expenses:

Source: "Coping with Poverty: Working-Poor Families in Georgia." The Center for the Study of Social Policy, Washington, D.C., July 1984.

Figure 8–4. Income and Expenses as Percent of Total Income

At the time of the interview, the families' budgets were lean. Most could not meet their monthly expenses on the $400 to $600 they received in income. As a result, they had to do away with certain items that most people take for granted. For example, 30 percent of the families did not have a telephone in their home and had to use a neighbor's phone or the nearest pay phone. Over half the families did not own a car or truck, despite the fact that most lived in rural areas where there was no public transportation. Consequently, they had to rely on relatives or friends to drive them to the store, to doctors' appointments, and, in many instances, to work.

Almost all the families (82 percent) had run out of money within the past year. For some women, this was practically a monthly occurrence no matter how hard they tried to budget their money. When this happened, the mothers would try to borrow money from family or friends or they would simply do without until their next paycheck. Several of the women noted that they tried to stick to a policy of never borrowing except from family members and only then when they were absolutely sure they could repay the money with their next paycheck. Reliance on family was also strong in times of financial crisis; many of the women went to stay with their parents when they ran out of money, and several borrowed money from their ex-husbands' mothers.

Furthermore, one-third of the families had run out of food completely within the past year. When this happened, the mothers would try to borrow food or money or turn to a food pantry for donations. Again, relatives were the first people turned to when the mother had no more food. Most took their families to their mother's or sister's to eat for a few days; some had their mothers send canned food through the mail or by bus; others went fishing or crabbing whenever the cupboard was bare. For many, though, running out of food meant eating nothing but bread and peas for days.

Finally, many of the mothers simply could not pay all of their monthly bills. As a result, 15 percent had had their utilities cut off within the past year for delinquent bills. Thus, almost one family in seven had gone without electricity or gas because it could not pay its bills. When this happened, the mothers again tried to borrow money. Some temporarily moved in with their parents; a few turned to old electric heaters when their gas was turned off; and still others applied for emergency fuel assistance.

Because of these financial problems, 38 percent of the families had accumulated bills that were more than two months overdue. These bills averaged $421, and the majority of them were for medical care. Table 8–5 shows the number of women who had various types of overdue bills and the amounts owed. Over half the women with overdue bills owed money for medical care, averaging $492. Several mothers had medical bills for $2,000, $3,000, and $5,000, not a surprising fact considering today's medical costs for emergency or hospital care. Without medical-care coverage, there was no way these mothers could repay such large medical bills, and so bills went unpaid.

Not only did the mothers run up unpaid medical bills, but since the loss of Medicaid, half reported they could not afford needed medical care for themselves and their children. Untreated gynecological problems were common, as were children's diseases. One woman noted that when her son needed emergency medical care for a high fever, "I had no Med-

Table 8–5
Overdue Bills (*N* = 79)

	Percent	Average Amount Owed
Rent	9%	$305
Electricity	19	77
Telephone	14	78
Medical	55	492
Other	45	238

Source: "Coping with Poverty: Working-Poor Families in Georgia." The Center for the Study of Social Policy, Washington, D.C., July 1984.

icaid and had to use my income tax money." Others could not get needed eyeglasses for themselves or their children because they could not afford them. As one woman noted, "I can't afford a doctor's care anymore; now I have to use home remedies."

In addition to compiling overdue bills, half the women owed money that they had borrowed for loans or installment payments. Forty percent of the women who had loans or installment payments owed money to a bank or finance company; 56 percent owed money to some lender, such as a store; and 4 percent had borrowed from relatives. Twenty-six percent had car payments for which they still owed $1,770 on average; 24 percent had furniture payments averaging $340; 17 percent owed money for appliances averaging $270; and 5 percent owed an average $461 for consolidated loans they had had to take out to help pay bills in general.

The overdue bills and loans illustrate the double bind these women were in: they did not have enough money to pay their bills so they had to borrow and pay finance charges, thereby paying money in interest and pushing them further into debt.

Because of their tight budgets, most of the families had little or no money left over each month with which to buy such items as clothes. Sixty-one percent of the mothers obtained used clothes from friends and charities for themselves and their children. A new pair of shoes was a major expense for these families. Many went to rummage sales to buy clothes for their children and household items they needed. Furthermore, one-quarter of the mothers got old produce free or at reduced prices from their grocer so that their children could have the fruits and vegetables that they could not otherwise afford.

In sum, one year after the federal government withdrew these families' welfare grants and Medicaid coverage, their financial prospects were bleak. Most were unable to stretch their limited incomes to cover basic living expenses. As a result, they had accumulated large overdue bills (primarily medical because they no longer had Medicaid coverage); they sometimes ran out of food at the end of the month; and they rarely could afford the luxury of buying clothes for their children. On top of this, the mothers felt all the normal strains of raising children and maybe more strain than most families, where two parents were available to supervise the children.

With the absence of what had been a small but steady source of income support and medical coverage, the families now faced increased unpredictability and instability in their already turbulent lives.

Maggie Silverwood complains she never has enough time to spend with her three children. It's all she can do to cook them dinner when she comes home from work before collapsing herself. Maggie had to arrange for Tiffany, her four-year-old, to stay with Maggie's mother since she could no longer afford day care while working as a cashier at a fast-food restaurant. She tries to get to her mother's several times a week to see Tiffany, but her work shifts are irregular.

Lately Maggie is having difficulty with her fifteen-year-old son Rob:

> It all started when the coach called me one night and asked me to come to school to talk to him and Mr. Douglas (the principal). I took off early that Friday and went down there. They were real nice. They told me Rob had been skipping school and not going to practice. And then he was caught forging a check. And the next thing I know he'd broke his collarbone riding some boy's motorcycle.

Looking to the future, Maggie holds on to hope:

> Pretty soon, the children will be old enough to help themselves. I have to think on the positive side. I just feel things will be better in five years. We all have our dreams—maybe, I'll move, or remarry, and someday have a regular home life. If not, I just pray my children end up better off than I am.

Notes

1. News Conference with President Reagan, 4 April 1984.
2. Unpublished data from the Georgia Division of Family and Children's Services.

Part IV
Lessons for the Future

9
Lessons from OBRA

As we have seen, the administration claimed that its AFDC policies saved needed money, increased administrative efficiency, and curbed abuse by cutting off high earners who did not need assistance. In chapter 7, we documented the cost savings resulting from OBRA. Yet we also showed in that chapter that much of even these claimed cost savings may have been illusory in the long run, when families return to the rolls at higher grant levels and when offsetting costs in other related programs are considered. Thus the justification of OBRA as a cost-cutting measure is a dubious one at best.

This failure apparently stemmed from the federal government's misunderstanding of how federal requirements affect state and local programs and how these requirements can in turn be affected by state and local actions. OBRA's goals for federal fiscal control, for example, could have been achieved in other ways that would have been both more direct and more certain to achieve the desired cost savings. For example, the federal government could have simply decreased the federal matching percentage for AFDC benefit payments across the board and allowed states to decide how to cut their programs. This would involve a simple decrease in the current matching formula so that the federal share of AFDC payments would be lowered evenly across all states. A second option would have been for the federal government to completely federalize the program. This would mean that the federal government would establish uniform eligibility requirements and a national minimum benefit level. This would be the most direct way of controlling federal costs, for the federal government would have complete control over who gets what benefits nationwide.

As for the claim that OBRA enhanced administrative efficiency, chapters 5 and 6 indicate that the opposite was actually true. Administratively, OBRA created more problems than it solved. State welfare agencies faced huge difficulties in carrying out the new rules quickly; most were unable to put in place assessment procedures to gauge the effects of the new policies. At the local level, caseworkers had to recalculate grants according to new formulas and had to review monthly reporting forms that they used to review only quarterly. Clearly, the new rules did not make administrators' jobs any easier.

In one area, however, the OBRA changes have had the dramatic effect expected of them: they were extraordinary in their impact on families and in the degree of change they provoked in the basic goals and structure of AFDC. As described earlier, one of OBRA's purposes was to eliminate assistance to those who could help themselves (that is, work) and provide assistance only to those who were "truly needy" (presumably those families in which no one could work).

The attempt to eliminate families with earned income from the rolls had the clearest impact. By far the majority of cases terminated by OBRA involved families who had earned income, as documented in chapter 7. Yet the administration's action to remove earners appears to be an example of overkill. To eliminate assistance for the very few high-income cases on the rolls, the administration terminated benefits for hundreds of thousands of families, some of whom were only marginally above, and most of whom were well below, the poverty threshold. As we showed in Chapter 8, women in Georgia with average incomes of only $447 were cut from the rolls.

The effect of these changes is to withhold assistance—even small amounts of assistance—from low-income working families. Despite the low level of earnings for most of these families (the median of each state's average monthly earnings for AFDC families prior to OBRA was only $363—about three-fifths of the minimum wage), the policies introduced by OBRA held that these families did not need assistance. Put another way, public support for their work effort was withdrawn, and the families were left to fend for themselves.

The wisdom of this policy can be debated on many grounds. At this point it is sufficient to note that the policy may be shortsighted even on OBRA's own terms. If these families are unable to "make it" in economic terms, they may ultimately require more in public expenditures, not less. If their children incur educational deficits or health problems that are even less likely to be remedied because of the fewer resources available to the family, the long-term costs become even greater. Thus, while OBRA did succeed to some extent in cutting caseloads and costs in the short run, it may prove shortsighted in the long run.

OBRA's effects in reality were quite different from what the administration claimed. The 1981 changes pushed more families into poverty and made already poor families even poorer. Most important, the cuts withdrew vital health-care coverage from the families affected. When historians look back on OBRA, they are likely to judge it as an unprecedented shift in welfare policy.

President Reagan's AFDC policy changes, President Carter's Program for Better Jobs and Income, and President Nixon's Family Assistance Plan all sought to restructure the nation's public-assistance system.

President Reagan's "welfare reform" was enacted, while both FAP and PBJI did not survive the legislative process. The differences among the approaches to welfare reform help explain these successes and failures.

First, both FAP and PBJI would have restructured AFDC by establishing minimum incomes for the needy, broadening eligibility to encompass needy persons excluded from assistance, and preserving the work-incentive character of the program. President Reagan's reforms did the opposite: they mandated maximum income ceilings for workers who were deemed needy, restricted eligibility, and eliminated the work-incentive provisions after four months of work. Second, while FAP and PBJI envisioned a more direct federal role in public assistance by standardizing state welfare programs, the 1981 initiative indirectly expanded the federal role. The federal government ignored the historical intergovernmental partnership that characterized AFDC by tinkering with the details of program administration traditionally left to the states.

The 1981 federal AFDC changes marked a fundamental shift in the nation's approach to public assistance. But they did not constitute welfare reform as most people have come to view the meaning of *reform*. To be sure, the administration's goal of saving money went hand-in-hand with its goal of paring down the welfare rolls. To the public, the budgetary goal was couched in terms of a major welfare-reform effort to rid the welfare system of cheaters and return AFDC to its rightful place as a small program serving only the truly needy.

Ironically, the same issues that contributed to the Reagan administration's success were instrumental in dooming FAP and PBJI to failure. FAP and PBJI were, for the most part, acceptable as welfare-reform plans but unacceptable as budget practices. The reason for this is what some have called the "welfare conundrum." This conundrum revolves around the fact that it is relatively costly to provide both adequate benefits to nonworkers and an adequate work incentive for workers. Since we want workers to be better off than nonworkers, providing adequate benefits for nonworkers entails providing costly supplemental benefits to workers. The traditional solution to this dilemma is to strike some sort of compromise, providing limited benefits to nonworkers and maintaining an adequate work incentive. Both FAP and PBJI, in their attempts to increase assistance to nonworkers and still maintain a work incentive, were positive welfare reform efforts—but relatively costly ones.

President Reagan's approach to welfare reform was radical: instead of dealing with both halves of the troubling dilemma, it purported to resolve the welfare conundrum by eliminating the work incentive. But the administration did not deal with the adequacy part of the equation by "re-targeting" funds from the working recipient to the nonworking recipient. Despite much rhetoric about re-targeting, the administration did not increase in any way funds for the truly needy. Nor did it make any effort to assist by any other methods the low-income workers it terminated from AFDC. Thus, President Reagan's changes were welfare reform only in the literal sense that they changed the existing welfare structure. If welfare reform means, as it must, that work is rewarded while those who cannot work are protected from destitution, then the 1981 changes were certainly not welfare reform. Instead, the Reagan administration's reply to the welfare conundrum (which requires a trade-off between minimally decent benefits and fairness to low-income workers) was to discard both sides of the equation. This can hardly be considered a positive reform.

In this context, the only plausible interpretation of OBRA is that the administration simply wanted to save money by cutting families off welfare—strictly a budgetary goal. The 1981 changes reflect no regard for the history and complexity of the federal-state partnership that characterizes AFDC. Nor did the administration take the time to find out who would be cut off AFDC and what effect such an action would have on these families.

Previous welfare-reform efforts have always specified the number of families at each income level that would receive increased benefits and the number that would receive reduced benefits. In this way, issues of fairness and equity could be measured and openly discussed. The 1981 changes in AFDC neglected or perhaps intentionally disregarded this critical step, and were apparently instead founded on the basis of a rather crude philosophical notion that the working poor should be "weaned" from dependency.

When the disparity between intention and achievement is as great as it is with OBRA, the basis for the policy change must be questioned. Clearly, change was not based on hard evidence. No one in the administration seemed to take into account the complex character of AFDC as a joint federal-state venture. While the administration asserted that it wanted to eliminate the high earners from the welfare rolls, its method of doing so also knocked off many families who were earning subminimum wages. For example, while a few of the families terminated in Michigan and New York City earned wages between $800 and $1,000 per month, families in Georgia were terminated by the same rules at monthly earnings of $400. The administration apparently did not differentiate between high- and low-payment states, so that many families in the low-benefit states had their grants terminated at subpoverty incomes.

Moreover, the OBRA policy changes were not based on a thorough understanding of the day-to-day workings of AFDC. OBRA's planners failed to anticipate even in small measure the way the AFDC changes would be implemented in states and localities. Nor were the changes grounded in knowledge of the poor served through AFDC. The 1981 law was driven by the budget process and reflected very little understanding of the daily life of low-income women. This human factor—an adequate understanding of the situations, aspirations, and frustrations of low-income families—is essential if policy development is to be effective.

Given such serious shortcomings in the conception of OBRA, what can be concluded about the motivating force for these changes? At best, the changes reflect a basic misapprehension of how the program actually works; probably, they were driven by ideological motives that simply overrode any facts which stood in the way.

Aftereffects

The findings from several research studies, including the center's survey of families in Georgia, suggest that the federal budget cuts created great financial hardship for working mothers and their children, making already poor families even poorer. One of the best gauges of the morality of a society is how it treats its most disadvantaged members. This treatment is not simply measured in dollars but in the fairness and decency of that society's policies.

The AFDC changes affected families that were indisputably poor, families who struggled every month to make financial ends meet. It is painful for most of us to imagine losing 10 percent of our family income, but it is much more painful for families who have nothing to spare. Through all the debates over the "deserving" versus the "undeserving" poor, over work disincentives and the work ethic, and all the predictions and counterpredictions of savings, we cannot ignore one fact. There are hundreds of thousands of women working and striving to provide an adequate standard of living for themselves and their children: the undeniable impact of the federal cuts was to increase their burden and push them deeper into poverty.

Perhaps the most damaging effects of the AFDC cuts were on the children in these families. Even before the cuts, there was little money available for clothes, school supplies, and toys, and sometimes there was not enough for food. After the cuts, there was even less. Moreover, the new AFDC rules in 1981 and subsequent ones enacted in 1982 denied eligibility to children over age eighteen (or age nineteen for full-time students about to graduate), eliminating benefits to students through age twenty-one. The administration is now proposing the age limit be sixteen. It is ironic that a program designed to help needy children is continually reducing aid to the very group it purports to serve.

Not only did the cuts put vulnerable children more at risk, they also tightened the welfare trap around them. The cuts reduced the children's options when they reached age eighteen by diminishing family income and terminating aid earlier in a child's life. At the same time, they offered nothing positive to the youth at age eighteen, no ladder to help him or her climb out of poverty. Without a job and with no continued financial aid, it is no wonder the cycle of poverty perpetuates itself.

The budgetary whirlwind that often dominates Washington causes policymakers to think of costs in strictly monetary terms. But policies can be costly in terms of principle, dignity, and fairness, as well as pragmatic long-term investment. The new AFDC provisions did not merely create an additional burden on children and on women who work and raise families, they also undermined the fundamental principle of the work ethic. The changes reduced the income differential between nonworking AFDC recipients and low-income workers. Our nation's policies should ensure that those who work are better off than those who do not work. That was the purpose of the work-incentive provisions of AFDC that President Reagan eliminated.

With hindsight, the most alarming aspect of the OBRA changes may be what they reveal about the way in which AFDC policy is now being shaped and what this portends for the future of the program. As we have seen, the OBRA changes were enacted in 1981 with little sense of how they would be implemented by state and local governments and with even less knowledge of how they would affect recipients. Terminations and benefit reductions were allowed to proceed in a haphazard fashion across states. Documentation of the effect of each OBRA provision was sporadic, making assessment of results difficult. Despite the lack of data, however, the administration claimed that OBRA had been successful, and further program cutbacks were enacted in subsequent years.

The experience with OBRA could be accepted as business as usual in the implementation of federal policy. After all, few federal programs have been launched with an accurate appraisal of their likely impact. Moreover, lack of data is a chronic problem in the evaluation of social welfare policies. Yet the Reagan administration apparently did not even try to estimate the policies' effects before they were enacted. The OBRA AFDC changes were not isolated instances of "belt-tightening" or even of "reining in" an out-of-control entitlement program, because prior to OBRA, AFDC costs and caseloads had been stable for several years in spite of a deep recession. Instead, as we have indicated, OBRA represented an attempt to diminish the welfare system. It did not pursue the desired goals of welfare reform, that is, greater equity in benefits and assurance of a minimum level of benefits for all those in need; instead, OBRA sought to alter the AFDC system in fundamental ways.

Looking to the future, the issue is whether this manner of formulating and implementing AFDC policy will continue unchanged. If a national commitment to minimal income support for families and children is to be maintained, this model of policy development is unacceptable. It is not rooted in knowledge of program operations, and it does not seek even basic evidence of its successes or failures. What is needed is policy development that more accurately reflects the reality of AFDC as it works today and that assesses new policies by scrutinizing their impact on families. To urge that AFDC policy be developed in this fashion is not necessarily to urge more spending, nor does it represent a desire to return to the status quo. Change in AFDC is needed and long overdue. But to allow it to proceed without regard for its damage to the structure of the present income-assistance programs and with no consideration of how it affects families and children now and in the future is a shortsighted and irresponsible way of spending the public's money. The nation's history of measured but incrementally progressive efforts to meet the needs of disadvantaged families requires that we act more responsibly in the future.

Postscript

Because federal policy-making is a dynamic process that is constantly in motion, new legislation often becomes quickly obsolete. And so is the case, in part, with OBRA. Several of the 1981 AFDC policies were changed in 1984. Congress enacted a new set of AFDC rules as part of the Omnibus Deficit Reduction Act of 1984 that took effect on October 1 of that year. These latest changes were positive attempts to reinstate benefits for some working mothers and to ease the transition from welfare to work for others. However, they will only reinstate a very small proportion of the families who lost their AFDC grants in 1981 and 1982. Among the new rules are the following:

The eligibility ceiling is changed from 150 percent to 185 percent of the state need standard. This will allow a few more working families to qualify for aid.

Whereas OBRA counted an Earned Income Tax Credit as income when determining AFDC benefits whether or not the recipient received the tax credit, the new law counts the EITC as income only when it is actually received.

The new law allows all working mothers to deduct $75 as a standard work expense, whereas previous law allowed $75 only for full-time workers and $50 for part-time workers.

The new law provides for a twelve-month continuation of the $30 disregard. Under OBRA, the disregard expired after four months. Note, however, that the one-third is not continued, only the $30.

Congress also took steps in 1984 to ease the transition from welfare to work for some of the families terminated under the 1981 rules. Under the Work-Transition Allowance, some families who lost their AFDC grants in 1981–83 because of the expiration of the $30 plus one-third disregard may now become eligible for Medicaid. However, the implementation proceedings required to recertify a family are complicated, and it is likely that only a small number of families will be able to take advantage of this provision.

If there is any lesson to be learned from these 1984 changes as a reaction to OBRA, it is that policy analysts and policymakers must understand the detailed technicalities of AFDC and related programs if they are to change the system. They must also be able to translate theoretically the technical changes into operation so they can estimate their impact on people in both the short and long term before the changes are actually made. As we have seen, this is the largest failure of the 1981 AFDC policy changes.

10
Short-Term Reforms

As we have shown, President Reagan's response to the problems of the welfare system was to terminate welfare assistance to families who work but cannot earn sufficient wages to raise themselves out of poverty. The idea of removing the working poor from the welfare rolls would not be so bad if we substituted another mechanism that provided them with some assistance and maintained a work incentive. But the Reagan Administration did not do this. It simply cut the families off welfare. Period.

Yet President Reagan's actions are not the only reason we need to reform our welfare system. Our welfare programs and policies were already badly in need of reform even before his 1981 policy changes. AFDC is a prime example. It has, through the years, become overextended. AFDC was designed not to prevent poverty but rather to help already poor families cope with economic hardship. Yet it has become a catch-all program charged with remedying a wide variety of social ills. It has acquired these functions because of the inadequacies of other social systems that should be integral parts of an overall approach to reducing poverty. AFDC has assumed responsibilities that more appropriately belong to the employment and training programs, the education system, health institutions, and vocational rehabilitation programs. The welfare system should be the safety net of last resort, not the first line and only defense against poverty. By subsuming the failures of other systems under welfare's administrative umbrella, welfare has become inconsistent in its objectives and difficult to manage. The welfare system's accountability for a whole host of social problems has masked the fact that the resulting costs are not strictly welfare costs. Instead, they are the price of the failure of our economy and of other service agencies to effectively provide low-income individuals with the means to become economically self-sufficient. President Reagan's policy changes only made matters worse.

There are a number of steps we could take in the near term to help the working poor. Instead of trying to reinstate the AFDC policies as they were before 1981, we should start from where we are now and devise new strategies to help the working poor through means other than AFDC. In other words, we should use President Reagan's actions to positive advantage: simplify AFDC by using it primarily for nonearners and create new avenues to assist low-income working families. It is the second half of this strategy that President Reagan and his staff ignored. While low-income workers do not necessarily need permanent welfare benefits, some income supplementation is essential if these families are to rise out of poverty or at least provide a decent standard of living for their children. A work incentive is also needed to encourage families to take and keep low-paying jobs. In short, new strategies are needed to help the working poor, and these should not be merely a return to what existed before 1981.

One way to provide income supplementation to the working poor while maintaining a work incentive is through the tax system. There are a number of specific changes that could be made in the existing tax code to help the working poor. This is a particularly feasible strategy for 1985 and 1986 because tax reform is now on the legislative agenda. Several congresspersons have introduced tax bills to simplify the current code, as has the administration. Each of these bills promises to help supplement the incomes of low-wage earners to some degree by exempting them from federal income taxes.

Targeting aid to low-income working families through the tax system is important today not only because their AFDC has been withdrawn but because low-income working families in general have had to pay an increasing share of their income in federal taxes. At the same time President Reagan cut AFDC benefits in 1981, Congress enacted at his request a tax bill that failed to adjust for inflation for low-income earners and thereby increased the income-tax burden for the poor. Prior to 1981, Congress had tried to exempt families with incomes below the poverty level from paying federal income taxes (although they did have to pay payroll taxes). It has generally been agreed that families earning poverty-level wages should not be obligated to pay income taxes.

Since 1981, families well below the poverty level have paid federal income taxes. Figure 10–1 shows the tax threshold in relation to the poverty standard over time. While the poverty threshold is indexed for inflation, the tax threshold—the point at which workers must begin paying taxes—is not. Throughout the sixties and seventies, the income tax threshold was always close to or higher than the poverty threshold, meaning that most families below the poverty line did not have to pay federal income taxes. From 1975 through 1980, taxpayers did not start paying taxes until their income reached nearly $1,000 above the poverty standard. Beginning in 1981, however, the tax threshold dropped well below the poverty level. From 1981 to 1984, taxpayers with incomes

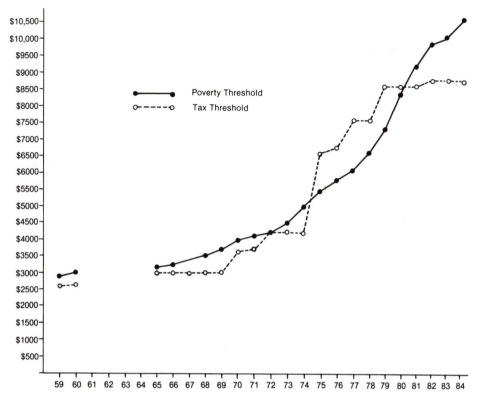

Figure 10–1. Tax Threshold and Poverty Threshold, Family of Four, 1959–84

$1,250 below the poverty line had to pay federal income taxes. By 1984, a family of four began paying taxes when their annual income reached $8,783, even though the poverty level was $10,613. Thus the percentage gap between the tax entry point and the poverty level was 17.2 percent. This gap is expected to increase to 21.5 percent in 1986. This is the largest gap between the tax threshold and the poverty level since before 1959.[1]

Furthermore, families with poverty-level incomes had to pay up to two or three times as much in federal income and payroll taxes as they paid six years ago. An analysis by the Committee on Ways and Means in the U.S. House of Representatives showed that federal income and payroll taxes increased by 280 percent between 1980 and 1984 in constant dollars for a family of four at the poverty level. In 1980, a family of four with earnings at 75 percent of the poverty level received $239 back from the IRS because its refundable tax credits exceeded its tax liability. Yet, by 1984, the same family had to pay $44 in federal taxes, for an effective tax increase of $283 (in constant dollars).[2]

There are three strategies that could be used to provide assistance through the tax system to working families now that AFDC is denied them. One strategy is to expand the existing Earned Income Tax Credit to supplement the wages of all low-income working families; a second is to make the existing child-care tax credit refundable and thus available to low-income families; and a third is simply to raise the tax threshold so the poor and the near-poor do not have to pay taxes. In addition, we suggest a fourth strategy to provide Medicaid to uninsured low-income working families whether or not they receive AFDC. Together, these strategies would provide needed income supplementation and health care to the working poor and offer a work incentive that at least makes working more profitable than not working. Following is a description of each.

Expanding the Earned Income Tax Credit

The EITC is an existing refundable tax credit available to families who have children and who earn less than $11,000 per year. Any qualifying family that files a tax return can receive it. Working families with annual incomes up to $5,000 are eligible to receive 11 percent of their income as a tax credit. Families with annual earned incomes between $5,000 and $6,500 receive the maximum credit of $550. Benefits then taper off on a sliding scale to zero at an annual income of $11,000 (see figure 10–2).

Because the credit is refundable, families do not have to pay taxes to claim it; the IRS will send them a check for the amount due them even if they do not owe taxes. The EITC was introduced into the tax system in 1975 to offset payroll taxes as a way of rewarding people for taking and keeping low-paying jobs. It has been modestly expanded only twice since 1975 and, consequently, the value of the credit has eroded on account of inflation. Figure 10–3 shows the erosion in the value of the EITC between 1975 and 1983. Even though the credit was increased by 25 percent in 1978, its value fell 33 percent because of inflation by 1983. Moreover, the credit is still not indexed to keep pace with inflation and thus further decreases in value with each passing year.

To help low income working families with their greater tax burdens and the withdrawal of public assistance, the EITC should be expanded

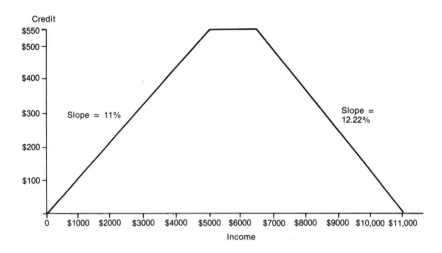

Figure 10–2. The Earned Income Tax Credit

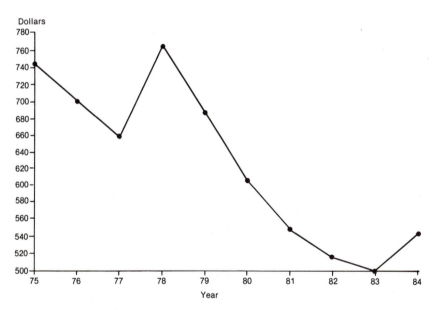

Figure 10–3. Earned Income Tax Credit, 1975–83

and indexed to keep pace with inflation. Specifically, five changes should be made. First, the EITC should be made available to all low-income persons, not just to families as it now is. By tying eligibility to family status, single individuals and childless couples are ineligible for the credit. It should be expanded to provide income supplementation to *all* low-income workers regardless of their family status. Second, eligibility for EITC should be broadened. This means raising the cut-off point above $11,000. Third, the amount of the credit should be expanded. Currently the maximum is only $550 per year, or about $46 per month. This amount should be raised to more adequately supplement the incomes of the working poor. Fourth, the EITC should be indexed to keep pace with inflation. This would prevent Congress from having to increase the credit through legislation every couple of years and ensure that the value of the credit would remain constant.

Finally, EITC should be adjusted by family size to give greater benefits to larger families. If we are to use EITC as the primary means of income supplementation for the working poor, it must provide adequate assistance for larger families, who obviously need more money with which to live.

Figure 10–4 provides an illustration of how the EITC could be expanded to meet these five principles. Benefits would vary by family size. The plateau would remain constant between $7,000 and $8,000. This means that all families, regardless of size, would receive the maximum credit when their income was between $7,000 and $8,000. The eligibility cut-off point would be $16,000 for all families, although families at this end of the eligibility scale would receive very small benefits.

Single individuals would receive a tax credit of 10 percent of their income up to $7,000; their maximum credit would be $700 per year. Two-person families would receive a maximum credit of $840 per year; three-person families, $980; four-person families, $1,120; and five-person families, $1,260. These levels would be indexed to keep pace with inflation each year.

Clearly, this proposal will require new money. Depending on the exact variations chosen, we estimate it might cost anywhere in the range of $4 to $6 billion in new federal funds.

Making the Child-Care Credit Refundable

A second strategy for targeting assistance to the working poor also involves the tax system. The child-care tax credit currently provides a tax credit to families for child-care costs up to $2,400 per child. To be eligible, both parents must be working, or, in the case of a single-parent family, the parent must be working. Families with incomes below $10,000 are eligible for a credit of 30 percent of the first $2,400 in child-care expenses for one child and up to 30 percent of the first $4,800 for two

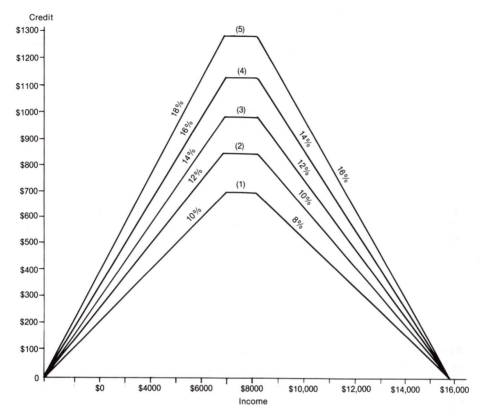

Figure 10–4. Proposed EITC

or more children. For each $2,000 in family income above $10,000, the credit is reduced by 1 percent until it reaches 20 percent when family income is $30,000. Above $30,000, the credit remains constant at 20 percent of expenses up to the limits mentioned previously.

However, the credit is out of reach of many low-income earners because it is not refundable and is therefore not available to low-income families who do not earn enough to pay taxes. Unlike the EITC, which provides a cash payment to eligible families irrespective of their tax liability, the nonrefundable child-care credit is merely subtracted from tax liability. For those with no tax liability, the credit is worthless. For those with a tax liability that is less than the child-care credit, the part of the credit that is above the tax liability cannot be used. Making this credit refundable would help many low-wage earners, thereby offering another positive incentive to work.

The problem can be illustrated with a hypothetical example. Mrs. Smith works forty hours per week at minimum wage, $3.35 per hour. Her gross annual income is $6,968, assuming she is not sick and takes no vacation. Because she spends $90 per week in child care for two of her three children, she is technically eligible for a child-care credit. The credit is calculated as 30 percent of her annual child-care costs because her income is below $10,000: 30 percent of $4,680 = $1,404. But Mrs. Smith's income is low enough that she does not have to pay federal income taxes. Consequently, she does not receive the child-care tax credit even though she is technically eligible for it.

Consider a contrasting illustration. Mrs. Johnson earns an annual salary of $20,000 and pays the same child-care costs of $90 per week for her youngest daughters as Mrs. Smith does. Mrs. Johnson is eligible for a child-care credit of 25 percent of her child-care costs: 25 percent of $4,680 = $1,170. Because Mrs. Johnson's income is high enough that she must pay federal income taxes, she receives the child-care credit. She simply deducts $1,170 from her federal tax liability and pays the difference, if any, to the IRS. The only difference between Mrs. Johnson, who receives the tax credit, and Mrs. Smith, who does not, is that Mrs. Johnson's income is high enough that she must pay taxes. The credit is thus somewhat perverse: it is unavailable to those who need it most.

Most of the low-income working mothers who lost their AFDC because of the 1981 policy changes did not earn enough money to be liable for federal income taxes. As a result, they cannot benefit from the child-care tax credit, which, while small, would at least help them pay the annual costs of child care when they work. As we saw in chapter 8, the costs of child care presented a problem for many of the mothers in the study, often forcing them to turn to relatives and other inexpensive forms of care. A tax credit, if made refundable to these low-income mothers, would help the unlucky mothers who do not have a relative or friend to care for their children.

Raising the Tax Threshold

Expanding the EITC and making the child care credit refundable would achieve one of the stated goals of tax reform: that of increasing equity, but they would not necessarily make the tax system simpler than it currently is. President Reagan has consistently repeated two goals of tax reform: equity *and* simplicity. One way to accomplish both of these goals would be to raise the tax threshold. By raising the income level at which people begin paying federal income taxes, working poor persons would be able to keep a larger portion of their earnings.

To raise the tax threshold, Congress could simply increase the zero-bracket amount. This is a flat amount of money ($2,300 for a single taxpayer and $3,400 for a married couple) that is exempt from federal income taxes. It is available only to taxpayers who do not itemize deductions. Thus, taxpayers who do not itemize pay no tax on the first $2,300/$3,400 of their taxable income. Raising the zero-bracket amount would be an efficient way to target tax relief on the working poor because it is available only to people who do not itemize deductions— generally those with lower incomes. The current zero-bracket amount for single persons would have to be almost doubled and the married couple amount increased by 41 percent to raise the income tax thresholds above the poverty line. Under several of the pending tax bills now before Congress, no one with incomes up to 100–130 percent of the poverty line would have to pay federal income taxes.

Raising the tax entry point would allow the poor and the near-poor to be free of federal income taxes (although they would still have to pay payroll taxes). This action is a form of income supplementation that is free of the stigma attached to the welfare system. Raising the tax threshold may be the simplest and most equitable means of achieving long overdue tax relief for low-wage earners. Alone, it is not a sufficient response to the problems created by the 1981 AFDC cuts, but in combination with an expanded EITC and child care credit, it would reinstate the work incentive.

Providing Medical Assistance Regardless of AFDC Status

Another near-term reform, although not through the tax system, is to revise the Medicaid program, which now finances medical care for welfare recipients. To be eligible for Medicaid, one must (with a few exceptions) be eligible for cash welfare assistance, either AFDC or SSI. This requirement creates at least two perverse incentives. First, it makes it less desireable to get off welfare since working one's way off welfare often means losing Medicaid coverage. Second, if one loses one's job and health insurance, one must (in many states) leave one's family in order to have the family qualify for welfare and Medicaid.

Like AFDC, Medicaid eligibility also varies significantly from state to state. A mother of two who earns $500 a month would qualify for Medicaid in California, New York, Connecticut, or Illinois, but not in Texas, South Carolina, Virginia, or seventeen other states. The result is that about half of the population in poverty has no health insurance. Many of these families are working. The National Center for Health

Services Research, a division of the Department of Health and Human Services, reports that since so many families lost Medicaid because of the 1981 AFDC cuts, "the percentage of working poor who lack any health insurance is probably higher than our 1977 estimate of 22 percent."[3] Most of the AFDC families were left without Medicaid when they lost their AFDC grant, and few had health insurance through their jobs. This increased the pressure on both public and private hospitals to accept "charity care." This in turn contributed to rising private health-care insurance premiums for others.

One solution to this problem would be to break the linkage that now exists between Medicaid eligibility and receipt of welfare cash assistance, and restructure Medicaid uniformly to protect individuals and families with incomes below the poverty line. This would enable low-income working families no longer eligible for AFDC to still receive Medicaid. As shown in chapter 8, many families in the Georgia study felt that the loss of Medicaid was more devastating to the family's well-being than was the loss of cash. Many had been unable to afford needed medical care when they lost their Medicaid. Providing them with Medicaid would enable them to obtain medical care when they or their children become ill—a vital necessity for two-thirds of the sample that did not get health insurance through their job.

In some states, families who do not qualify for AFDC may still get Medicaid under the state's "medically needy" program. In these states, a family may qualify for Medicaid if it is poor and if it has high medical expenses even though it may not qualify for AFDC. The medically needy program is an explicit recognition of the fact that not all poor families are eligible for AFDC. Many do not qualify for AFDC because they do not meet the family composition or assets requirements or because their income is slightly over the eligibility ceiling; yet, these families cannot afford to pay their medical bills—bills that can quickly exceed their resources.

It is these families, most of whom can be classified as the working poor, that need health insurance. Providing them with Medicaid unlinked to welfare would not only enhance their well-being but would alleviate some of the work-disincentive effects of OBRA. If low-income working families knew they could still get Medicaid even though they no longer received AFDC, they would be assured that they could be as well or better off financially than if they did not work and received only AFDC and Medicaid. In other words, offering them Medicaid would make work appear more worthwhile when compared to not working.

Health-care needs do not simply disappear when not provided for. Health-care costs for the indigent not covered by Medicaid are absorbed by county and other public hospitals as well as by private hospitals, which spread those costs to other patients. In fact, uninsured persons usually have higher health-care costs because they postpone treatment until a condition that might have been remedied through preventive care requires more substantial care, such as hospitalization. We have evidence that preventive health care is successful in reducing infant mortality. It is likely that providing Medicaid coverage to working-poor families would also prove a wise financial investment in the long run.

Justification for Changes

The cumulative impact of these four modest strategies—an expanded EITC, a refundable child-care credit, raising the tax threshold, and reform of Medicaid—would help the working-poor family provide for the basic necessities of living. Let us return to the hypothetical example of Mrs. Smith, who works at minimum wage, earning $6,968 annually. Under President Reagan's policies, Mrs. Smith must support herself and her three children on her earnings plus $1,430 worth of food stamps plus $530 in EITC, or a total of $8,928, which equals about 84 percent of the poverty threshold. If we expand the EITC as proposed above, she would receive $1,120; if the child-care credit were made refundable, she would receive another $1,404. Her total cash income would then be $10,922, or 103 percent of the poverty threshold. And more important, she would now have Medicaid to pay for needed medical care for her family. Thus the proposals outlined above would bring this hypothetical family above the poverty threshold. Although Mrs. Smith would not benefit from raising the tax threshold because her earnings are low enough to already be exempt from federal income taxes, other families with wages between $8,783 and $10,613 who now pay taxes would be relieved of this burden.

There are at least seven advantages of the above four proposals over the current system that make them important for policymakers to consider. First, the proposals would make working families better off than nonworking families. This gets to the heart of the work ethic and the crux of the problem with President Reagan's 1981 policy changes, which have had the opposite effect. Providing income supplementation to low-income working families through the tax system and offering them health insurance through Medicaid would ensure that they have higher disposable incomes than nonworking families. This principle must be reflected in public policy. It is an essential ingredient to a rational public policy course, just as other financial incentives are central to our economic system.

Second, these proposals would resolve the AFDC "notch problem" in the right direction. AFDC allows one working-poor family to have more income than a neighbor family earning the same wages that does not qualify for AFDC. President Reagan's response was to cut the income of those slightly better off so both families now had the same amount of money. If we instead supplemented the income of both working families in poverty through the tax system rather than AFDC, the families—both of whom are poor—would have equal incomes, only it would be at the level of the higher family income instead of the lower. Thus, the proposals would eliminate the inequity of the AFDC program—the so-called notch problem—while at the same time rectifying President Reagan's harsh solution.

Third, as implied previously, the four proposals would transcend the limited eligibility specifications in AFDC, thereby targeting assistance to a broader population of poor families. Cash assistance through EITC and protection from federal income taxes as well as health insurance through Medicaid would be provided to everyone with incomes under a designated level. In this way, more poor people who need help will receive it, and conversely, fewer will fall between the cracks, unable to obtain needed assistance. Furthermore, the current AFDC incentive for families to "break up" in order to receive aid would be eradicated for the working poor. Currently, in half the states, two-parent families are ineligible for AFDC and can get aid only if the husband leaves. If all persons could receive aid through the tax system and through Medicaid, married or not, there would be no financial incentive for mothers and fathers to separate. Either way, they would get the same amount of assistance if both worked.

Fourth, by broadening the population base and using the tax system, the new proposals would provide assistance without the stigma of the current welfare system. This is a clear advantage to poor families, who do not like to admit they receive welfare. Instead, they could fill out their tax return in the privacy of their own homes and not have to "show" anyone else that they receive government assistance. At present, many middle-income families proudly use the child-care credit; there would be no stigma for low-income families to do the same.

The fifth advantage of using the tax system to supplement the incomes of the working poor and provide them with Medicaid coverage is that it takes some of the burden off the welfare system, shrinking it to the residual program that President Reagan sought. AFDC could then become a much simpler program primarily for the nonworking poor. It would no longer have to be all things to all people. If AFDC were focused on the nonworking family, there would not be the terrible administrative nightmare for caseworkers that working families now pose. AFDC would be strictly a program to *ameliorate* poverty, while the tax system would be used to *prevent* poverty through income supplementation for the working poor. Moreover, by focusing solely on nonworking families, the issue of adequacy, which historically has taken a back seat to the work-incentive issue, could be addressed. As long as the EITC provided higher disposable incomes for working families than AFDC provides to nonworking families, AFDC benefits could be raised. A national minimum benefit could be established for all nonearners, guaranteeing them a uniform payment throughout the country. At the same time, two-parent families in which the principal earner is unemployed should also be made eligible for AFDC in all states instead of just the half that now provide for such families.

Sixth, income supplementation through the tax system would promote uniform assistance throughout the country, eliminating the inequity that currently exists among states with respect to AFDC benefits. We showed the extreme variation in AFDC benefits across states in chapter 2. In contrast, federal cash assistance based on income would be entirely equitable; a family in Mississippi earning $5,000 per year would receive the same amount of income supplementation as the family in California earning $5,000.

The final advantage of the tax system proposals is that they could be administered far more efficiently than AFDC now is. The tax credits have a proven track record. Administration of the tax credit or of the tax threshold is relatively simple; there are no caseworkers filling out lengthy interview forms to determine eligibility. The wage earner simply fills out his or her tax return, documenting gross income, and a tax table shows the corresponding amount of the credit. Similarly with the child-care tax credit, the working parent has only to compute his or her credit and include it on the tax return. This would be considerably more efficient and simple than the current AFDC system.

For all these reasons, the four proposals outlined above would make for a better system than what was in place before 1981. But they are even more urgent in the wake of President Reagan's actions because they would once again restore a work incentive while providing needed assistance to low-income earners. Once we have helped the working poor through the tax system, we can turn our attention toward making the welfare system for nonworking families more adequate. As the analysis in this book has shown, we are currently in a situation where incremental changes made in 1981 have made the welfare system progressively more irrational and less adequate. There is no excuse for government policy in a civilized society like ours to be callous and indifferent to the needs of the poor, just as there is no excuse for the 1981 OBRA changes—an unworkable set of policies that were hastily conceived with little understanding of AFDC.

Yet these suggestions, important as they are for the near term, are only incremental reforms that will do little to prevent poverty in the long run. These short-term strategies should be pursued, but we should at the same time undertake longer-term reforms that seek to prevent poverty at its roots: with young children.

Notes

1. *Taxing the Poor,* The Center on Budget and Policy Priorities, Washington, D.C., April 1984, 3.
2. Subcommittee on Oversight and Subcommittee on Public Assistance and Unemployment Compensation of the Committee on Ways and Means, U.S. House of Representatives, *Families in Poverty: Changes in the Safety Net,* 20 September 1984.
3. *Health Care of the Working Poor,* National Health Care Expenditures Study, National Center for Health Services Research, Public Health Service, U.S. Department of Health and Human Services, 5 October 1984, 10.

11
Shaping a Long-Term Perspective

The growth in poverty since 1981 has been accompanied by a
noticeable shift in public attitudes and policies toward the poor.
In a few short years, the Reagan administration has moved us
away from the view of public support and assistance as a clear public
responsibility with corresponding individual rights and entitlements to
the more narrow concept of a restricted safety net. The direction of this
change raises important philosophical questions for the future.

The debates on the federal budget and on reduction of the federal
deficit have obscured the shift in our social welfare programs. More than
budget cutting occurred between 1981 and 1984—government responsibility for the poor was fundamentally redefined. Since the 1960s, the
stated goals of federal policy have been to reduce poverty and to improve
the conditions associated with it—poor health and nutrition, inadequate
housing, lack of education, limited skills and access to employment opportunities. Consistent with these goals, government has spent increasing
sums on income support, food stamps, Medicaid, subsidized housing,
employment and training programs, health, social services, and other
categorical programs to improve the conditions of the disadvantaged.
President Reagan cut these public expenditures and, more basically, restricted public responsibility for these efforts. This shift may, in the long
run, be more significant than the immediate pain caused by budget cuts.
As we move away from a theory of social rights and legal entitlements
for assistance, we also undermine the recourse that individuals now have
to challenge reductions in benefits or to pursue political strategies to
increase their life opportunities.

From a public policy perspective, it is clear that the Reagan administration's changes were not guided by any new strategy either for reducing poverty and meeting the essential needs of the poor or for
addressing basic issues regarding the allocation of scarce federal, state,
and local resources. No new goals have been set for ensuring even the
minimal well-being of low-income families and individuals.

President Reagan's policies reflect the philosophy that government
bears little or no responsibility for disadvantaged citizens. This philosophy is certainly evident in the case of working-poor female-headed fam-

ilies, as we have documented in this book. But it also applies to other groups. Poor households receiving food stamps have had to make do with less. Many students are in jeopardy of no longer qualifying for student loans. Farmers are witnessing the foreclosing of farms because farm price supports have lapsed. Victims of discrimination due to race, disability, or gender have found the administration deaf to their pleas. Hundreds of thousands of physically and mentally disabled adults have had their Social Security disability benefits terminated. And thousands of people formerly working in public jobs became unemployed when CETA was halted. All of these groups are casualties of conservatives' largely successful attempt to get government out of the business of mitigating hardship. According to this line of reasoning, the social Darwinian doctrine of survival of the fittest seems to mean that government should not intervene to enhance the well-being of disadvantaged persons. Presumably, that task should be left to private charities, voluntary efforts, and the individuals themselves.

Escaping the Budgetary Stalemate

President Reagan has been able to carry out this radical philosophical shift through a careful but transparent strategy of manipulation. In his bid for the presidency in 1980, he campaigned on the promise of balancing the budget by 1984. He contended that, if elected, one of his first objectives would be to bring spending in line with revenue. But since being elected, President Reagan has done just the opposite. He has used the goal of a balanced budget—laudable but simplistic in and of itself— as a rationale for cutting social programs. He has repeatedly refused to allow revenue to be raised, and he has insisted on costly defense buildups regardless of whether the increased spending will actually fortify our national security. At the same time, President Reagan's 1981 tax bill has been labeled "corporate welfare" because the huge tax breaks that he granted to corporations have greatly reduced the corporate income tax. In 1952, corporations paid 25 percent of all federal revenues. By 1980, even before President Reagan's tax breaks, the proportion had dwindled to 12 percent, and by 1983, it had declined rapidly to 6 percent. As a result of these extraordinary tax breaks and special preferences, many corporations now pay no federal income taxes. A study of 250 American corporations from 1981 through 1983 revealed the tremendous windfalls experienced by some companies.[1] A full fifty-one percent of the companies studied paid *no* federal income taxes despite profits of over $57 billion in at least one of the three years between 1981 and 1983. For example, General Electric received $283 million in tax refunds between

1981 and 1983 while earning domestic profits of $6.5 billion; Boeing Company received $267 million in tax benefits or refunds while earning $1.5 billion; and Dow Chemical Company received $223 million in benefits or refunds while earning $776 million in profits. Five other companies received over $100 million each in tax benefits or refunds despite profits totaling $7.6 billion.

Despite the fact that in 1982 Congress revoked some of the 1981 tax cuts, data for 1983 show that the reforms still left massive tax breaks for corporations. In 1983, 67 of the 250 companies studied earned profits of $14.7 billion but paid no federal income taxes and claimed rebates totaling over $1 billion. In short, the highly paid business lobbyists won their budget fights, creating an even greater deficit, which in turn exacerbated the need to reduce the federal budget deficit through spending cuts. Conservatives and liberals alike knew that the poor are not organized, often do not vote, and have no highly paid lobbyists as corporations do. With little voice and no political or economic clout, the poor were left as the victims of the president's economic program.

In short, President Reagan began the most costly arms buildup in the country's history and gave business the largest tax breaks ever offered in any single year. He then said he would not raise taxes to pay for these new expenses. The American public applauded and elected Ronald Reagan to a second term in an overwhelming landslide over Walter Mondale, who promised to raise taxes. The Reagan agenda had been set and little room was left to maneuver. In our acknowledgment of the defense buildup and our desire not to raise taxes, the public has bought into the argument that the only way to reduce the deficit and enhance our economic prosperity is to reduce government's role in assisting the disadvantaged and to cut spending for social programs.

In 1985, when pressure to reduce the deficit has taken on historical proportion, President Reagan flatly refuses to consider raising revenue through taxes. This is in spite of the fact that in 1984, President Reagan announced he intended to simplify the tax code, which over the years has become a nightmare of entanglements. The terms of the debate have been defined: the alternatives of raising taxes or slowing the defense buildup are excluded, and we are thereby once again forced to accomplish deficit reduction goals at the expense of the poor.

The intended goals of the president's economic strategy has been to use the deficit (which he has escalated to unprecedented proportions) to force spending cuts in a narrow portion of the budget. By declaring defense cuts as well as tax increases off limits, President Reagan has forced the social programs serving the most vulnerable to absorb the brunt of the federal budget cuts—all in the name of decreasing the role of government. In doing this, he has pitted one advocacy group against another. By limiting budgetary debates to a small portion of the entire budget and forcing some amount of spending cuts within it, otherwise natural allies have become competitive in budgetary battles. The strategy can be described as "divide and conquer," and the result has been the massive budget cuts in social programs that the Reagan administration sought from its inception. Instead of banding together to fight cuts in *any* social area, individual interest groups have fallen victim to the premise that since some social spending must be cut, they must protect their individual interests at the expense of another group. It may be that unnatural allies form coalitions in the coming years to successfully force a new agenda.

As long as we succumb to President Reagan's ploy of keeping the debate of taxes separate from that of spending, we will find ourselves in a no-win situation of having to cut budgets further. This was, of course, the decision of the majority of the electorate in the past two elections. What has not yet been made clear to the public, however, is that the only way to pursue goals of equity and adequacy is to break out of this forced limitation. We are, in effect, refusing both to face up to the basic responsibilities of the federal government and to consider revenue-raising measures to support these responsibilities. Instead, we have allowed government aid for the needy to be withdrawn, federal support for urban areas to be curtailed, and mass transit subsidies to be slashed, among other actions, thereby ignoring difficult questions of governance. President Reagan seems to want to turn back the clock to a time when the individual was supreme and government had little responsibility for providing assistance to individuals.

The Breakdown of Rational Policymaking

The Reagan administration's budget cuts have dramatized the vulnerability of low-income individuals and families. For years, evidence has indicated the need to reexamine our approaches to poverty and to rethink strategies for reducing poverty. The Reagan administration did not invent dissatisfaction with the current maze of welfare programs, nor was it the first to identify past failures to alleviate dependence. Policy analysts, advocates, and clients have for years recognized the serious and, some say, intractable problems in our current system of income and in-kind supports for the poor. We have, over time, developed an intricate web of categorical programs. There has never been a successful attempt to create a coherent set of programs that work together to meet the needs of low-income people and families and to help them become self-sufficient. Instead, we have a patchwork of multiple and uncoordinated programs with large cracks through which people fall.

Furthermore, the existing maze of categorical programs has become so incomprehensible that it takes an astute technician to ascertain how each one operates and how one relates to another. The client rarely understands the rules of one program, let alone several. Over the years, as needs-tested programs have been more precisely targeted on the so-called truly needy, they have become increasingly technical and difficult to understand for the average taxpayer. Yet instead of trying to make welfare programs more humane and coherent, President Reagan has exploited the situation, making them worse instead of better.

One of the dangerous results of this evolution is the breakdown of rational policy-making. Because social programs are so complicated, policy is dominated by anecdotes. If the facts are too many and too complex to grasp quickly, policymakers become vulnerable to accepting catchy anecdotes—many of which are inaccurate—as the basis for policy decisions. Liberals and conservatives alike resort to oversimplifications in order to portray their vision of what is wrong with an existing program or policy.

A prime example of the anecdotal approach to welfare reform was demonstrated by President Reagan when he spoke of a man in the grocery line paying for an orange with food stamp coupons and using the change to buy vodka. Another was his comment on the exorbitant federal moneys spent on mass transit, when he exclaimed that government could afford to provide every resident in one city a limousine for a day with the money spent on the transit system. Such anecdotes quickly capture the alleged evils of a program by portraying an easily identified image. To the uninformed public, the anecdote then takes on a life of its own, conveying an entire ideology—in these cases, a negative portrayal of all 12 million households receiving food stamps and of public mass-transit subsidies. But the anecdote may be factually incorrect, as is the case in the two just mentioned. Food stamp rules allow a maximum of 99 cents in change to be given to any customer, hardly enough with which to buy vodka. And President Reagan was comparing the costs of limousines for *one* day with the total capital construction costs of a permanent transit system. The impression left by the anecdote is used as the basis for major program changes even though data consistently prove that the anecdotes are usually inaccurate or that they reflect isolated cases at most.

The way President Reagan conducts the public's business inhibits the intellectual community from thinking about long-term responses and stifles new initiatives. Since taking office, the president has cut back on research, curtailed information systems and reduced aid to education, all in the name of getting government off the backs of the people. As a result, policy analysts spend all their time reacting to whatever new budget-cut crisis is being created at the time. We need instead a vision of what we want our society to look like in the future. We must look beyond current budget cuts if we are to achieve a better world—one in which the federal government explicitly maintains responsibility for the disadvantaged.

Toward Long-Term Poverty Prevention

We need new long-term strategies for better governance. To continue the subject of government policy used in this book, let us examine briefly the subject of long-term poverty prevention. What does it mean to develop a strategy of poverty prevention? The dictionary defines prevention as "stopping or keeping from happening by some prior action." We can easily comprehend the prevention of a specific disease, like measles, through the creation and use of a vaccine. But it is much more difficult both conceptually and practically to prevent poverty, a condition that is neither easily defined nor easily treated. What actions can we take to forestall poverty or what obstacles can we put in its path?

On one level, a long-range poverty prevention strategy will require that we make economic decisions more explicitly than we do now. Government is inextricably involved in aiding the private sector through subsidies to private industry, bailouts, or special tax treatment. Unfortunately, these decisions are made arbitrarily and are not part of an overall economic plan. Government awards benefits to those with the most power. As we saw in chapter 4, even David Stockman acknowledged that the poor had no voice in budget matters. We need to develop mechanisms at the community level to translate government policy into positive action. This is needed if we are going to succeed in devising long-range solutions to the problem of poverty. We can continue to abdicate this responsibility and limp along from one economic crisis to another, or we can mobilize our nation's considerable talents to devise an investment strategy for preventing poverty in the coming decades.

President Reagan's actions have perhaps given us the opportunity to revise the way we make long-term choices concerning the poor. The fact that current welfare policies are untenable may force policymakers to think carefully about what government's responsibilities should be and how government can best provide assistance to the poor. Clearly there are limits on what government can and should do, but we have not defined those limits precisely enough just as we have not articulated what government should do and how it should go about doing it.

The kind of long-term reform of the welfare system that is needed would not be reform of just AFDC; it would involve many other programs, some old, some new, designed to give children the opportunity to be self-sufficient when they become adults. For example, we must

> use what we have learned from the successes of Head Start and give young children from disadvantaged families special attention *before* they enter school so they can succeed better when they get there;

> restructure our education system to prepare youth better for life after high school;

> use the federal government to promote better dropout prevention programs;

> encourage creative work-school programs for high school students from disadvantaged homes so that the work experience they acquire while still in school will increase their chances of getting jobs after they graduate;

> prevent the escalation of homelessness by, among other things, halting the elimination of funds for housing subsidies;

> develop a new national policy to ensure the availability of affordable housing for all Americans; and

> continue mass-transit subsidies to unclog our highways and provide affordable transportation to city residents, including low-income persons.

New measures must be developed to encourage those not in the labor force to reenter the economy. Most important, youth training and employment programs must be strengthened and reshaped with a new urgency that recognizes the process of alienation experienced by many young people. Youth employment is not only an end in itself but a means to prevent the economic attrition of young men and women and to improve the structure and economic status of families. The list of what we need to do could go on and on.

Establishing a poverty prevention agenda is in the government's own self-interest, just as it was when the government bailed out Chrysler in order to enhance American productivity. The growing disparity between the "haves" and the "have-nots" is cause for serious concern; it threatens to perpetuate a two-society nation with a widening gulf between the poor and nonpoor. Without a new agenda, disadvantaged groups will continue to have little hope of attaining productive lives in an integrated society.

On the other hand, we probably cannot attain this goal within the confines of our existing economy. Government must stimulate new economic ventures so we have an expanding economy instead of a shrinking one. There are dozens of jobs that need to be done in our communities: roads need to be repaired, bridges need to be maintained, forests need to be thinned out or replanted, and elderly people need to be assisted in their own homes to prevent institutionalization, just to name a few. It seems entirely appropriate for government to promote such activities which are sorely needed and which would increase jobs and build a larger tax base at the same time. We can only afford a long-term poverty prevention agenda if we first create an expanding economy.

A new poverty agenda is urgently needed for the sake of the next generation. Today, 13.6 million children are growing up in poverty. For the federal government to neglect these children is not only reprehensible but also foolish. To deny opportunities to children is to impede their development into healthy and self-sufficient adults.

Because poverty is a national problem that cuts across state lines, eradicating it should be a federal priority. History has demonstrated that the private marketplace alone cannot solve the problems of poverty and should not be expected to. Similarly, state and local governments lack the resources and national leadership to tackle the problems of the poor by themselves. In the end, we must acknowledge that poverty is a responsibility of the federal government. This is not to suggest that the federal government can eliminate poverty on its own; it needs the cooperation of state and local governments to translate its commitment into reality.

In summary, we need simultaneously to pursue long-range prevention of poverty and near-term structural reform of our welfare programs. For far too long, these endeavors have been thought of as mutually exclusive. But the current status of AFDC policy urgently requires that we recognize the need for both by adopting a dual strategy. By initiating a long-range approach to the prevention of poverty, we must be clear about who will be helped. Our sights must be set beyond the current generation of adults and beyond current programs with all their deficiencies and inequities. It is the children of today and tomorrow who will benefit from a long-term prevention strategy.

Without a long-range vision, we will continue to use residual needs-tested programs to pick up the pieces of poverty after the fact. Traditional welfare programs do nothing to prevent poverty, and continuation of our historical welfare approach can only lead to more of the same: ever-growing, costly programs aimed only at ameliorating the effects of poverty. Policy analysts must use our detailed knowledge of current programs and policies to design both long-range prevention strategies and short-range programmatic reforms that go beyond abstract theorizing and incremental tinkering. Our ultimate goal is to create public policy that affirms a national commitment to provide increased opportunities for the poor in the near term, and to eradicate poverty entirely in the future.

President Reagan's actions may have had at least one fortuitous side effect: they have forced us to evaluate the question of whether we as a society can afford social and economic justice. The answer, upon careful reflection, must be that we cannot afford to ignore matters of equity and adequacy for the disadvantaged. Continuing along the path that drives our economy at the expense of social justice is morally unacceptable.

Perhaps the most essential element in the creation of a new long-range approach to assist the disadvantaged is an informed citizenry. The public needs to know how government policies are made and what effects specific policies have on select groups. We must make government accountable for its actions. We the public must become more sophisticated and vigilant if democracy is to prevail over government by the few for the few.

1. Robert S. McIntyre and Robert Folen, *Corporate Income Taxes in the Reagan Years,* Citizens for Tax Justice, Washington, D.C., October 1984.

Index

About the Authors

Tom Joe is director and founder of the Center for the Study of Social Policy, a nonprofit organization located in Washington, D.C., that conducts research and policy analysis of social issues. Since earning a master's degree in political science from the University of California, Berkeley, he has worked in a number of public human service agencies at the state and federal levels of government. He served as senior staff to the California Assembly Public Welfare Committee and was special assistant to the undersecretary of the federal Department of Health, Education, and Welfare during the Nixon administration. Mr. Joe has also worked as a consultant to the White House and to several executive agencies for the Carter administration.

Cheryl Rogers is a senior research associate at the Center for the Study of Social Policy. She has a master's degree from the University of Arizona. Ms. Rogers formerly worked as a research associate at the Urban Institute before joining the center when it was founded in 1979.